MUSICALS

MUSICALS

Daniel Cohen

GALLERY BOOKS
An Imprint of W. H. Smith Publishers Inc.
112 Madison Avenue
New York City 10016
A Bison Book

Copyright © 1984 Bison Books Corp.

Published by Gallery Books
A Division of W.H. Smith Publishers Inc.
112 Madison Avenue
New York, New York 10016

Produced by
Bison Books Corp.
17 Sherwood Place
Greenwich, CT 06830
USA

Printed in Hong Kong

1 2 3 4 5 6 7 8 9 10

ISBN 0-8317-6258-6

CONTENTS

ONE

Music and Film

Remember when Saturday afternoon meant the movies? Some loved comedies, some loved mysteries, but for many the big thrill came with the musical, the Hollywood musical. Run the words together, Hollywoodmusical, and you get a little tune. You can tap it, sing it, whistle it.

Sitting there in the dark, getting callouses on their knees from pressing them into the hard back of the seat in front, they would wait for the big event.

Anticipation has never been so sweet. Whether the screen came alive in a shimmer of silver or a blaze of glorious technicolor they were happy. For now there was a beautiful make-believe world where every few minutes somebody broke into song and where all the things they wanted in real life and never got came true on the screen.

We are going to look back on a lot of those old musicals and the newer ones as well. But what is a musical? Fans know by instinct. It isn't a movie with an occasional musical interlude. Early motion pictures were heavily influenced by vaudeville, with its wide variety of different acts, so musical numbers were frequently tossed into films to add spice. Take a look at some of the Marx Brothers movies. Except for Chico's and Harpo's comic routines on piano and harp you could chop out the songs. And despite the famous 'As Time Goes By,' *Casablanca* is by no means a musical.

Page 1 : Streisand sings 'Before the Parade Passes By' in this production number from *Hello, Dolly!* (1969).
Page 2 : A scene from *Fame.*
Previous pages : Julie Andrews in *The Sound of Music* (1965).
Opposite : Annie and Sandy in *Annie* (1982). Aileen Quinn played the title role in the musical based upon the cartoon strip. It was director John Huston's first musical.
Inset : Mitzi Gaynor, as Nurse Nellie Forbush, in *South Pacific* (1958), surrounded by a chorus of sailors.

42nd Street is. Singin' in the Rain is. So is Annie. And, to be a little idiosyncratic, maybe even Saturday Night Fever. What do all these films have in common? They rise and fall on their musical scores. Without their music, where would these films be?

Of course, the very word musical tends to conjure up a certain image. By and large, musicals are not message movies, although ask yourself whether there isn't a message in West Side Story or South Pacific. 'Let Me Entertain You' could be the motto for most movie musicals.

The entertainment can be light and frothy, bubbling with wit and foolishness. It can showcase singing à la Jeanette MacDonald and Nelson Eddy, or dancing as in the case of the inimitable Ginger Rogers and Fred Astaire. It can have comedy. Didn't we all laugh our way through Danny Kaye's Up In Arms? Never forget that the words musical and comedy go together. People said they were going to see a musical comedy long before they learned to say just musical, because on Broadway musical and comedy were synonymous for years. And Hollywood has based a lot of its musical films on Broadway shows.

Musicals can illuminate the talents of many, as in a review, or let a single star shine. Think of Barbra Streisand in Hello Dolly. It can be sad, a three handkerchief job, like Carousel. You can skate through one if you're Sonja Henie, or swim through one if you're Esther Williams.

Sometimes the costumes and sets are dazzling. Remember The Red Shoes? On the other hand take a look at the early 'let's put on a show, kids' musicals Judy Garland and Mickey Rooney did. They were pretty simple.

And, speaking of kids, the Hollywood musical has been

Above : Carmen Jones (1950) starred Dorothy Dandridge and Harry Bellafonte. It was an update of the Bizet opera and contained an English libretto by Oscar Hammerstein II. Both of these popular singers' voices were dubbed.

8

one of the premier vehicles for child stars. Shirley Temple's tapping toes and golden curls are legend. Then there's Margaret O'Brien and Deanna Durbin. American audiences loved little girls.

Black performers, often barred from other kinds of films, appeared frequently in musicals. Who could ever forget Dorothy Dandridge in *Carmen Jones*?

Musicals can be an exercise in nostalgia like *Grease*. Or they can be written for nonmusical talent, as in the case of Rex Harrison in *My Fair Lady*. In the remake of *Pennies from Heaven*, Steve Martin stars in a Hollywood musical that downs Hollywood musicals. Disney made them with animation. Liza Minnelli made them a family tradition. Busby Berkeley immortalized them.

It took a lot of people to put them together. They needed music, lyrics, dialogue, plots, choreographers, dancers, singers, actors, costume designers, set designers, cameramen and countless others. They were the biggest, most expensive Hollywood ventures. And they paid off. They were wildly popular. America hummed their tunes and worshipped their stars. They set audiences sighing over romance. Ah, those beautiful Goldwyn girls. And sent them home with a happy ending.

They were our great escape. And though they could be silly, once in a while they were stupendous. How about *The Wizard of Oz*? So let's take an in-depth look at them. It is fitting that Hollywood recently remade *The Jazz Singer*, for we must go back to the days when talkies began. Sound brought Hollywood the musical.

Welcome to *The Sound of Music*.

Above : One of MGM's top musical teams was Mickey Rooney and Judy Garland, shown here with Tommy Dorsey, his trombone and his band in *Girl Crazy* (1943). The plot concerned a rich young Easterner (Rooney) whose father exiles him to a small school out west, and the Gershwin score was first rate.

Opposite far left : The ending of the knife fight in *West Side Story* (1961). The film was an adaptation of the Broadway musical which was an adaptation of Shakespeare's *Romeo and Juliet*, transferred to the slums of New York with the Montagues and Capulets replaced by the Sharks and the Jets— two rival street gangs. The score was by Leonard Bernstein. *Above center :* *Singin' in the Rain* (1952) was the story of the silents-into-talkies panic in Hollywood during the late 1920s. Here is one of the impressive dance routines with Gene Kelly and Cyd Charisse.

9

TWO

In the Beginning

I t had been a silent place, the old movie theater. Well, not really. The tinkle of the piano had provided accompaniment. But pictures were just that, pictures, a feast for the eyes. You could be deaf and go to the movies but you had better know how to read.

On 6 October 1927 things changed. Al Jolson cried 'Mammy' in *The Jazz Singer* and took the audience at New York's Warner Theater by storm. Not that the original *Jazz Singer* was a musical, mind you. It wasn't even really a talkie. Most of it was silent. It wasn't even the first time sound was tried on film. But it was the first big commercial breakthrough, a response to Hollywood's major competitor, radio.

The bits of dialogue in *The Jazz Singer* caused a revolution, although for a while you got a strange hybrid. Joan Crawford's *Our Dancing Daughters*, 1928, is basically a silent musical with some sound effects thrown in. Universal's *Showboat* was given a quick bath of sound after it was made. And since early sound was technically difficult to achieve, even the best of voices in all films sounded squeaky.

Although Hollywood produced straight talkies the idea of 'singles' caught on from the first, even though audiences had to wait until 1929 to see their first true musical, *The Broadway Melody*.

After his success in *The Jazz Singer*, Jolson made *The Singing Fool*. In the midst of a plot so melodramatic the

Right : A scene from one of the all-star blockbuster musical reviews of 1930—*Happy Days*. Billed as a Fox Movietone Musical Romance, the picture featured almost all the contract players from that studio. Among them were Janet Gaynor, Victor McLaglen, Edmund Lowe and El Brendel.
Opposite inset : Jeanette MacDonald starred with Maurice Chevalier in *The Merry Widow* (1934). The film featured the grand old Franz Lehar melodies outfitted with new lyrics by Lorenz Hart.

Above: Al Jolson in *The Jazz Singer* (1927). As a story, it was not much, but Jolson's overwhelming stage personality shone through. The songs—among them such Jolson trademarks as 'Toot, Toot, Tootsie,' 'Mammy' and the Jewish prayer for the dead, 'Kol Nidre'—enchanted the audience. *Below:* Joan Crawford and Conrad Nagel in a tender scene from the extravaganza *Hollywood Review of 1929*.

theater must have been awash in tears, Jolson sang. Warner's made a bundle. The stage, or in this case, the screen, was set. George Jessel made *Lucky Boy* in 1929, finishing the picture with a song to mother. This sloppy tribute was followed by Morton Downey's *Mother's Boy*. He topped everybody else by singing to a mother close to death.

By now it was obvious that audiences were getting tired of mothers, although Sophie Tucker made her movie debut with a variation on the theme. Instead of singing to or about a mother, she was a mother, rejected by an ungrateful daughter in *Honky Tonk*, 1929. We see echos of this plot in the Betty Grable, Dan Dailey musical of 1947, *Mother Wore Tights*. As for the Jolson-Jessel-Downey style of film, well, sentimentality formed one of the basic motifs of Hollywood musicals for years, also reaching its peak in the 1940's, with films like *Meet Me In St Louis*, MGM's huge hit of 1944.

At first Hollywood limped towards its toetapping musicals via revues. These were closer to vaudeville shows performed in front of a camera than to consistent movies. *The Hollywood Revue of 1929* had Jack Benny as one of its masters of ceremonies, Marion Davies, Marie Dressler and Ukelele Ike (Cliff Edwards) doing 'Singin' In The Rain.' The movie was a mishmash of song, dance, comedy and even Shakespeare. It also had color sequences. It quite literally had everybody and everything except the kitchen sink.

Paramount on Parade followed suit in 1930, and something called, in those pre-television times, *Happy Days*. But the novelty was wearing off and the mere sound of the human voice croaking on the screen would no longer suffice. Enter Irving Thalberg, practically a kid, the boy genius of MGM. *The Broadway Melody*, a sweet story of two sisters seeking fame on New York's Great White Way, was born. This was MGM's first total talkie.

It was slangy, it was creaky, but it had some strong performances, was a top money maker and became the first sound film to win the Academy Award as best picture. It also set some precedents. The chorus girls were gorgeously clothed. The songs were good; 'You Were Meant For Me' became a hit. And Broadway, which Hollywood felt distinctly inferior to, was the place to set your story. In keeping with the spirit of the revue, musical numbers could be presented as lavish extras rather than arising from the story line itself, the play within a play approach. Compare this with the approach to a musical of the 1960s, say *West Side Story*, where the dancing springs from the plot itself, as rival gangs show off their talents as dancers.

A bunch of Broadway stage door musicals followed, *Broadway Babies*, *Broadway Scandals* and the first of the gold digger films, *The Gold Diggers of Broadway*, 1929. Basically, they had the 'You're going out there a lowly toad, kid, but you're coming back a star' story line or 'from rags to riches, if you've got good legs and take elocution lessons.'

Another trend was the operetta. This was meant to be a musical with class, although as in the 1929 *Desert Song*, which concerns the doings of a romantic bandit leader known as 'The Red Shadow,' we are reminded more of Valentino than Verdi. *The Desert Song* with score by Sigmund Romberg and Oscar Hammerstein II was the first full talking and singing operetta for the screen. It featured no less an actress than Myrna Loy as the exotic native girl, Azuri.

Operettas were often filmed in two-color technicolor but they lacked the lightness of touch of the Broadway Back Stage musicals. *The Vagabond King*, 1930, did introduce Jeanette MacDonald, however, one of the all-time great musical stars, and Warner's brought out a fresh and adorable *No, No, Nanette*. *Rio Rita* made its appearance and Flo Ziegfeld's fabulous Marilyn Miller came to the screen in *Sally*.

College campuses in the 1920s must have struck a lot of people as playgrounds. In Hollywood, students almost never hit the books. *Sweetie*, starring Jack Oakie and Helen Kane, was all about the trials and tribulations of a football team and the more famous *Good News* (MGM, 1930), showed everyone how to do 'The Varsity Drag.' Definitely, it was a more innocent age.

Sunny Side Up was Janet Gaynor's first real talkie. One of the best things about it was that, unlike so many musicals, it was written expressly for the movies, and wasn't merely a third-rate adaptation of a Broadway show. This represented a break from the traditional notion that you merely set up a camera and film a play. Gaynor is, as usual, the brave little sweetheart from the slums. She gets what she deserves, a millionaire. But she is winsome and the movie has appeal even now.

Top : A production number from *Hollywood Review of 1929.* The film was closer to a vaudeville show performed in front of a camera than to a movie with a consistent plot.
Above : The first American film made by the great French entertainer Maurice Chevalier was *The Love Parade* (1929). Here the threatening girl is saying, 'I'd rather see you dead than in the arms of another woman!'

One of the ornate production numbers from *Gold Diggers of Broadway* (1929).

It took a master to cope with the elements sound introduced—the great film director, Ernst Lubitsch. Best known for his sophisticated comedies and their faultless evocation of wealth and glamor, he was nonetheless a significant factor in the development of the early musical. Admirers and detractors alike had to admire 'the Lubitsch touch'.

In 1929 he was already a famous silent film director and he found the new art form of musicals dreadfully stodgy and lifeless. He wanted to bring wit, zest and sexiness to them. He paired a charming redhead, Jeanette Mac-Donald, with the great cosmopolitan star, Maurice Chevalier, casting them in his first talkie, *The Love Parade*. *The Merry Widow* is perhaps their most famous co-partnership. But they are also highly engaging in *One Hour With You*. Lubitsch's plots were sometimes foolish and a hindrance to his elegant style, but he pointed the way to a subtle low-key kind of musical rather than the brash sock-'em-with-everything style that tended to dominate the medium in the following decade.

Another major film director who became interested in musicals was King Vidor. Carrying his originality over from silents to talkies he made *Halleluja* in 1929 with an exclusively black cast. His use of work songs and spirituals, his brilliant sound effects and camera work, the intensity of the film, raise it above the ordinary.

Vidor was taking the musical into a new and more serious direction. In 1929 Helen Morgan appeared in another musical, Paramount's *Applause*, which also matched music with a story that didn't have a happy ending. Helen Morgan plays a burlesque queen abused by an ugly world. The director, Rouben Mamoulian, never let the camera lie. This is not a pretty movie though it was innovative in the use of techniques which would later be used in a lot of pretty films, for example, the handling of close-ups.

But despite these gems a lot of musicals were stiff and tedious. The public was no longer thrilled merely by the novelty of a voice singing. The audience wanted more. Unfortunately, musicals were still in the experimental stage and so by the early 30s were no longer pulling them in at the box office. Word was that the depression was killing them.

Actually the depression was going to glorify them. They were to rise to dizzying heights, far surpassing what they were in the beginning. They would become the perfect entertainment medium for hard times, big, bold, and totally un-Lubitsch.

But there is more than one road to greatness. The high-kicking platinum blonde musical of the 30s was about to make its debut. The best dancing ever. The best singing ever. And it all started with an innocent-looking little lady named Ruby Keeler who wore the biggest tap shoes in the world. She was the kind of girl you wanted to bring home to meet your mother. You weren't alone. Everybody fell in love with her in *42nd Street*.

THREE

Brother, Can You Spare a Dime?

They may have been singing it in the heartland of the Midwest and out on the Dust Bowl or in the Hoovervilles that dotted the railroad tracks, but the musical made Hollywood's 1930s theme song 'We're In the Money.' Darryl F Zanuck of Warner Brothers decided the time was right to make a really big splashy musical which would combine the best elements of the Broadway Back Stage genre. But it needed punch, it needed wow, it needed something special to bring in the audience. That something special turned out to be a musical director, one Busby Berkeley.

He was already well-known on Broadway, having gone west in 1930 to make *Whoopee* starring Eddie Cantor. With musicals in the doldrums he was about to return to the Great White Way when miraculously along came the chance to do *42nd Street*. Thanks to Berkeley and a marvelous cast the film was what we today would call a blockbuster. Sounds like the plot for a musical, doesn't it? Stars were born and if there is a Hollywood Hall of Fame in Heaven today, Berkeley is in it.

Aside from Ruby Keeler as the ingénue the movie had George Brent and Bebe Daniels, both veterans, Dick Powell, who had sung with a band, and an up-and-coming sexy starlet with a peppery personality, appropriately named Ginger. Miss Rogers was destined to become one of the hottest Hollywood musical stars ever.

Right : Dorothy (Judy Garland) and her friends about to enter the Haunted Forest on their search for *The Wizard of Oz* (1939). To Dorothy's left, the Tin Woodman (Jack Haley), the Cowardly Lion (Bert Lahr) and the Scarecrow (Ray Bolger). The film was the most expensive in MGM's first 15 years.
Opposite inset : Fred Astaire in one of the inventive routines in *Roberta* (1935), a movie that featured a score by Otto Harbach and Jerome Kern.

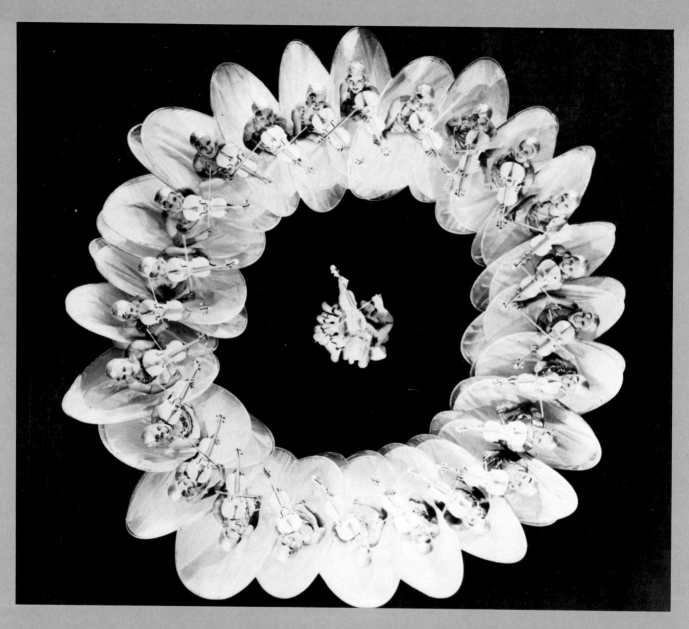

Opposite top : A Busby Berkeley trademark—chorus girls with unusual props photographed from above, from *Gold Diggers of 1933.*

Opposite bottom : *Gold Diggers of 1935* gave Berkeley a chance to direct an entire movie, not just the musical parts. Still, he did not stint when it came to the songs. He loved to move hordes of pretty girls around, individualizing them with a lot of close-ups, then bringing them together to form the parts into one gigantic whole. In this scene, the girls play separate pianos, merging finally into one huge piano.

Top : The two stars of *Gold Diggers of 1933*—Ruby Keeler and Dick Powell. This was her second film and his fifth.

Above : More Busby Berkeley routines were in *Footlight Parade* (1933). This is the 'By a Waterfall' scene.

Busby Berkeley was one of a long line of talents who understood that what the audience was seeing was shot through a camera. He knew you could create a visual fantasy if you used the camera in the right way. A perfectionist, he refused to let the film cutter tell him what to do. Instead he followed his vision, creating elaborate patterns, weaving his dancers into geometric shapes and forms. Thanks to him, the camera became a magic eye.

42nd Street appeared in 1933. As a tribute to its archetypal greatness we now have a hit Broadway musical based on it, a case of New York tipping its hat to Hollywood. Is there anybody in the world who doesn't know the plot? Director Julian Marsh (played by Warner Baxter) is a cynical old piece of tough shoe-leather putting on his last great show, *Pretty Lady*. He has to replace his leading lady with a sweet young thing with big soulful eyes (Ruby Keeler). Gee, she's just a kid right out of the chorus. Can she do it? Has she got the guts, the talent? Marsh works her like a dog, a Svengali to her Trilby. The dialogue fairly crackles, one gem of a cliche after another. Does our heroine rise to the occasion? Will her name shine in lights? Take an educated guess.

Nothing succeeds like success and nothing clones more imitations. After *42nd Street*, gaudy musicals were in. Ruby and Dick were paired once more in *Gold Diggers of 1933*. Ginger Rogers was back, too, a conniving little thing, eager to make it big. Her name in the film was Fay Fortune, proving that Hollywood figured subtlety was a waste of time. Something new was added, or should I say, someone. Joan Blondell provided sparkle and humor to the moving picture show. Busby Berkeley was given carte blanche and the dancing is, to say the least, amazing. The one serious note is Joan Blondell's rendering of 'Remember My Forgotten Man,' a reminder of the soldiers who fought in World War I and who were lucky if they could sell apples in the street in 1933.

Footlight Parade, another in the Powell-Keeler-Broadway mold, is important because it gave James Cagney his first singing and dancing role in the movies. Again, Berkeley made fireworks with tiers and towers of girls who looked like they were made of spun sugar. The way he used water in the number 'By a Waterfall' was a forerunner of Esther Williams' bathing beauty musicals of the 1940s.

Then came *Dames*. We meet much of the same cast and much of the same plot again. It doesn't matter. This movie is chiefly an ode to Berkeley's talent. Thanks to trick photography and crowds of chorus girls the audience could delight in the sensational choreography. Everything the depression was not, this picture is. *Dames* is fat and rich and gooey.

Gold Diggers of 1935 gave Busby a chance to direct an entire movie, not just the musical parts. Still, he does not stint when it comes to the songs, which most resemble a three-ring circus gone bananas. Busby Berkeley loved to move hordes of pretty girls around, individualizing them with a lot of close-ups, then bringing them together to form the parts into one gigantic whole. In *Gold Diggers of*

1935 the girls play separate pianos, merging finally into one huge piano. In *Gold Diggers of 1933* it was violins. When Berkeley thought flowers, the petals were girls.

Disciplined artist as he was in many respects, Berkeley was like a kid with an expensive toy. The best thing about *Gold Diggers of 1935* is 'The Lullaby of Broadway.' It's not just a song, it's the acting out of a little musical playlet, in this case a seamy New York, at its lowest, type of scene. It is reminiscent of the later 'Slaughter On Tenth Avenue' danced by Vera-Ellen and Gene Kelly in MGM's *Words and Music*, 1948, and was a common device in the musicals of the 50s.

Gold Diggers of 1937 revealed a tame Berkeley, a man with budget problems. He left Warners in 1939. Berkeley's achievement is enormous. His routines were never dull. They are popular to this day. The man's imagination was spacious. There was nothing petty or cramped about him. He would literally try anything.

If most of his numbers tend to be abstract and lacking in heart, well, so what? At least they aren't maudlin or overly sentimental. Their shiny glow makes us all believe that we are children set loose in a candy store with a pocketful of small change.

No one man, however, can write the history of an era and there were other careers besides Berkeley's. Powell and Keeler had other directors. In 1935 Ruby Keeler appeared in *Go Into Your Dance* with her real life husband, Al Jolson. Rudy Vallee, who was to hang around even after *How To Succeed In Business Without Really Trying* was made in 1967, was crooning his nasal numbers on screen as early as 1929. In 1934 he appeared with Alice Faye in *George White's Scandals*.

20th Century-Fox brought out *Stand Up And Cheer* in 1934 which trumpeted the notion that the depression was over, and gave Shirley Temple her first major moment on film, singing and dancing to 'Baby Take a Bow!'

But if the big fancy musicals like *Scandals*, pushing the extravaganza with lots of naughty sex, were in, so was the romantic tradition of operetta. Jeanette MacDonald was an established star before she teamed up with Nelson Eddy, although her career had taken a plunge when musicals went down in the very early 30s. *The Merry Widow*, 1934, sent her to the top again.

But her big smash hit came in 1935 when she appeared for the first time opposite a new talent, if talent be the word. Nelson Eddy was blond. He sang baritone. And he was an instant star. *Naughty Marietta* made more money than any musical up to that time. After that Jeanette MacDonald and Nelson Eddy were bound to be an onscreen pair over and over again.

Naughty Marietta was a relatively low budget film. Its director, Woody Van Dyke, was competent but not brilliant. The movie's plot is pure melodrama, but Jeanette MacDonald was an experienced professional and the Victor Herbert music appealed to the masses. Has 'Ah, Sweet Mystery of Life' ever sounded the same since? Nelson Eddy wasn't exactly lively but perhaps American

Opposite top : Ruby Keeler and her husband, Al Jolson, finally got a chance to star together in *Go Into Your Dance* (1935). The highlight was their singing and dancing in the number 'About a Quarter to Nine.'

Above : Alice Faye marries Rudy Vallee in *George White's Scandals* (1934). Behind Vallee is Jimmy Durante. Faye had once been a singer with Vallee's band and this was her first film. Its idiotic backstage plot seemed to propel an entertaining, expensive musical. The hit song was 'Oh, You Nasty Man.'

Below : Jeanette MacDonald and Nelson Eddy in *Rose Marie* (1936). In this film a young actor, in only his second picture, was tapped as a future star—he played MacDonald's brother and his name was James Stewart.

women found his stiff stoicism charming. Although Astaire and Rogers have endured, Eddy and MacDonald were the darlings of their era.

In 1936 they appeared together in *Rose Marie,* and this time they had a bigger budget, so the movie is more lavish than *Naughty Marietta.* To appreciate this film you have to see it as it was seen in 1935. This is the famous Canadian Mountie movie and later, more sophisticated, generations have made fun of it.

The plot is no dumber than many 'let's put on a show!' films. Unfortunately, it isn't any smarter either. Marie de Flor (Jeanette MacDonald) is an opera singer, strictly a high-class lady who goes to the wilds of Canada because her brother (Jimmy Stewart) is there, having escaped from jail and murdered a mountie. En route the fair Marie meets a handsome mountie (guess who) tracking down her brother. In this movie everybody wins except Jimmy Stewart. He's got to go to jail again. Message: Don't mess with a mountie.

Most of the songs are by Oscar Hammerstein II and Rudolf Friml and when they were first sung nobody laughed. To us it is very hard to take 'Indian Love Call' seriously. But that doesn't make us right and millions of people in 1935 wrong. It just means that the styles have changed.

Nelson Eddy and Jeanette MacDonald were trained singers. They were supposed to be bringing culture to the audience. Compared to them, Busby Berkeley, Astaire and Rogers and George White were low-brows. It was also okay to be absolutely drippingly romantic in 1935. People were not yet embarrassed by love. 'When I'm calling you-ou-ou-ou-ou-ou-ou', six ou's, count 'em, wouldn't cut the mustard in the 1980s but it set a lot of hearts pounding in 1935.

Maytime was next. Based on Sigmund Romberg's 1917 operetta, it was delightfully costumed, taking audiences into a never-never land of the Paris of Louis Napoleon where a young couple fell in love. Make-believe worlds of the past with their period costumes had a strong appeal to Hollywood audiences for decades. Critics loved *Maytime.* MGM raked in the big bucks.

Time could be stopped in the movies but time passed in real life and the duo's later movies began showing wrinkles. He grew fatter, leading some sneering critics to refer to him as 'The Singing Capon.' She grew too old to carry off an ingénue role. But they spawned an entire line of romantic operettas set in the past. One thinks of Kathryn Grayson and Mario Lanza in *That Midnight Kiss,* MGM, 1949, and *The Toast Of New Orleans,* 1950.

Jeanette MacDonald and Nelson Eddy's success made many a studio head decide to cast serious singers in movies. Grace Moore of the Metropolitan Opera made *One Night of Love* in 1934. Irene Dunne, a talented singer as well as actress, appeared in *Show Boat.* So did the extraordinarily gifted black singer, Paul Robeson. Ida Lupino appeared in a spoof of the MacDonald-Eddy tradition, called *The Gay Desperado,* 1936.

But, though they left their mark, we don't think first of Jeanette MacDonald and Nelson Eddy when we recall the glory years of the 30s' musicals. Another couple has taken first prize. Not much doubt about who they are. Introducing Miss Ginger Rogers and Mr Fred Astaire.

He was over 30, a not particularly good-looking song-and-dance man looking for a future star. She was a moderately well known starlet. Together they created the epitome of the 30s musical. Against Art Deco sets of velvet black, lustrous white, and champagne bubble silver they danced. And how they danced. It wasn't through the voices of trained singers in operettas, or through the spectacular staging of chorus girls, that the musical reached its greatest heights. No, it was through the feet of Fred Astaire and Ginger Rogers. Two pairs of tap shoes said it all.

It was 1933. The depression was at its nadir and RKO had just taken note of the cyclical return of the musical. They wanted a piece of the action, so in a speedy four weeks they put together a movie starring Dolores Del Rio called *Flying Down to Rio*. The best thing about it were Astaire and Rogers, playing characters named Fred Ayres and Honey Hale. When the dynamic duo did 'The Carioca,' charisma flashed on the screen. A year later they were given another vehicle, this time as stars. Originally called *Gay Divorce*, it arrived at movie theaters as *The Gay Divorcee*. The plot is silly. Most of their plots were surprisingly pre-adolescent for such clearly grown-up people.

The truth is, nobody in the audience gave a damn about the plots. They went to see them, to watch them dance. Oh, there was comedy, too. Erik Rhodes as the stage Italian, Eric Blore as the stage English butler, Edward Everett Horton doing his double takes and a very young Betty Grable who had been making movies since 1930.

The choreographer of *The Gay Divorcee* was one Hermes Panagiotopulos, better known under his professional name of Hermes Pan. He worked with the prancing pair in later films and deserves a lot of the credit for the wonderful dance numbers.

The Gay Divorcee sets the tone for all their movies. Fred, alias Guy Holden (where did they get their names?) sees Ginger and bang, it's love (read that sexual attraction) at first glance. He pursues her hither and yon through a glamorous resort hotel. She resists, but all you have to do is see them dance to know he'll get her. This is no Broadway Back Stage musical where dances have nothing to do with the story line. It is when Fred and Ginger dance that we see how they feel about each other. All the sensuality missing in the dialogue comes out as they dance to Cole Porter's 'Night And Day.'

This was a breakthrough for musicals. For the first time not the songs but the dances convey emotion. No wonder Fred and Ginger rarely even bothered with the obligatory Hollywood romantic kiss. They didn't need it.

In 1935 the dazzling duo made *Roberta* but it was Irene Dunne who had the lead in this adaptation of the Otto Harbach-Jerome Kern stage show. Fred is Huck Haines, Ginger is Lizzie Gatz, but she likes to call herself the

Countess Scharwenka. They steal the picture. Fred Astaire, with his thin voice and thinning hair, seemed to pass through a magic transformation when he danced. He became the most attractive, most elegant, most debonair human being on earth. If he'd danced with Helen of Troy it would have been hard to keep your eyes off him and on her so it's a tribute to Ginger Rogers that she not only didn't fade from view but added a tart glamor of her own.

The public liked what it saw and so in 1935 RKO gave them *Top Hat*, the sort of vehicle they needed. It is much more like *The Gay Divorcee* than *Roberta*. With its plot of mistaken identity and accidental confusion, RKO might have resurrected Bill Shakespeare to write the story line. Edward Everett Horton, Eric Blore and Erik Rhodes are there. Everybody seems to have money pouring from every seam of his sumptuous wardrobe. Venice looks as if it were built by a Miami Beach developer. Irving Berlin's music is great.

Fred dances his first solo of the film in the room above Ginger's. The noise bothers her as she lies in a bed that would have embarrassed Mae West. Thus, they get off to the usual antagonistic start. In 'Isn't This A Lovely Day' we get a chance to see Ginger dance in pants. She wears a riding habit. We get the banter in the words and the struggle in the dance. 'Cheek To Cheek' gives us the lust and tenderness as the two dance what they really feel. *Top Hat* is one of the best.

Follow The Fleet came next. There is some comic dancing in this one. Randolph Scott and Harriet Hilliard play supporting parts and we see Betty Grable again. But *Swing Time*, 1936, was a better movie. Some say it's Astaire and Rogers's top film. Astaire, as Lucky Garnett, has lost his money but not his tuxedo. Ginger, a dance teacher, still has the common touch that makes her so endearing.

Lucky meets Penny (Lucky Penny, Good Lord!) and after the requisite complications which give the pair an excuse to dance, there is a happy ending. Astaire does his blackface number, 'Bojangles of Harlem,' where he actually dances with shadows of himself, his first use of trick photography. There is the adorable satirical 'Pick Yourself Up' in which Fred pretends he can't dance, and the sweepingly expressive 'Never Gonna Dance'.

Shall We Dance?, 1937, has a score by the Gershwin Brothers, Ira and George. The best song and dance is performed on roller skates to 'Let's Call the Whole Thing Off.'

Top left : Fred Astaire and Ginger Rogers in *Follow the Fleet* (1936). It was the story of a song-and-dance man who joins the Navy when his girl breaks up with him. The couple was in top form, and there were such Irving Berlin songs as 'Let's Face the Music and Dance,' 'Let Yourself Go' and 'We Saw the Sea.'
Left : In *The Gay Divorcee* (1934), the Astaire-Rogers dance team finally got top billing. In this film they introduced 'The Continental.' The choreographer for the film was the extraordinarily fine dance master, Hermes Pan.

Fred and Ginger appeared in *Top Hat* (1935) in the same
year that *Roberta* was released.

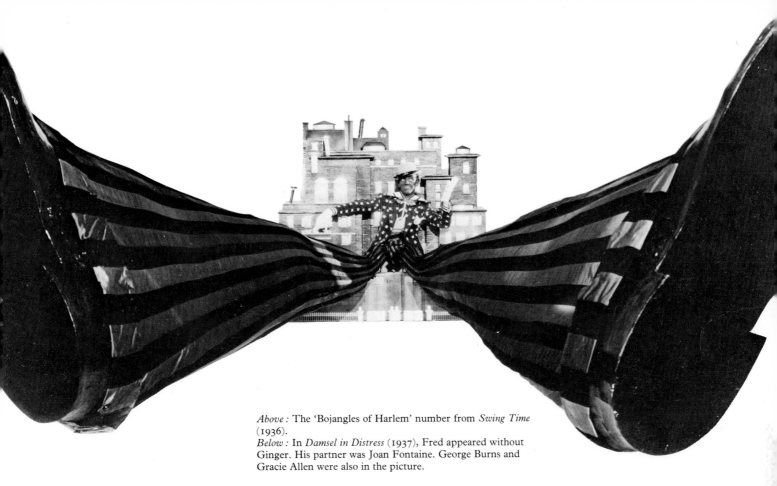

Above : The 'Bojangles of Harlem' number from *Swing Time* (1936).
Below : In *Damsel in Distress* (1937), Fred appeared without Ginger. His partner was Joan Fontaine. George Burns and Gracie Allen were also in the picture.

Nothing lasts forever and by now the pair was ready to split. Astaire did *Damsel In Distress*, 1937, based on the work of the master of humorous fiction, P G Wodehouse, and Rogers made *Vivacious Lady* the same year to emphasize her comic talents. The couple was back together for *Carefree* in 1938 but this film represented a big shift. Though it has music, it barely counts as a musical. In 1939, Fred and Ginger made *The Story of Vernon and Irene Castle* but this too is different, a bridge to the 40s. The light-hearted idiotic plot of their early films has melted away and the pair seem more mature and serious. There is a bit of a tear jerker ending. A decade later they made *The Barkleys of Broadway* with Oscar Levant, Billie Burke and Hans Conried. But that was accidental. *Barkleys* was

originally supposed to star Judy Garland and Ginger was brought in only when Judy was too sick to make the film.

After *The Story of Vernon and Irene Castle*, Fred and Ginger went their separate ways. Fred danced with Eleanor Powell in *Broadway Melody* of 1940. But despite the careers they pursued when they broke up, we still think of them together, ever young, dancing in some eternal crystal palace, making us forget for a little while that there's a Hooverville next door and we owe the landlord the rent.

Only one other musical star of the 30s had the same ability to take us out of ourselves. Even though she had golden ringlets and dimples, she wasn't a sex symbol. Her name stands for a nonalcoholic beverage to this day. Shirley Temple was 20th Century-Fox's pot of gold.

Oh, the studio had other stars. For instance there was Alice Faye. In *You Can't Have Everything*, 1937, she plays a granddaughter of Edgar Allan Poe, who, having written a meaningful play, watches it turned into a musical by Don Ameche. Alice Faye was a pug-nosed blond beauty whose star status lasted well into the following decade and beyond. Olympic figure skating star Sonja Henie made a series of successful skating musicals for 20th Century-Fox, including *My Lucky Star*, 1938, and *Second Fiddle*, 1939. When her film career was over she appeared in popular ice shows. Her smile glittered as brightly as her skates.

But nobody outdid Shirley. Born in 1928, she made her first movie in 1934. By 1937 she was making more money than any other singer-actress in Hollywood.

Her 'On The Good Ship Lollipop,' and 'Animal Crackers In My Soup,' are immortal. She was so famous you could buy a Shirley Temple doll, get a mug with her picture on it and read books about her presumably wonderful life.

What was the key to her success? Why did middle-aged ladies coo over her? Why was she the envy of every real life little girl in the world? Well, she was cute as the dickens. By our lights the curls and dimples seem a bit much. But just as romance was acceptable to the audience of the 30s, so was innocence. Shirley was the ideal babykins of a sentimental age.

Not only did she look like Cupid, she could sing and dance. Watch her tap routines in *The Little Colonel*, 1935, with Bill Robinson, no less. She was a good impressionist as she proved in *Stowaway*, 1936, where, with a boy doll attached to her toes, she even imitates Astaire and Rogers.

Besides her talent, her ability not only to be cute, but to project it, Shirley had something else—spunk and stamina. In her films she often overcame adversity. Unspoiled and good-tempered, she was a kind of noncartoon Disney type heroine. Depression audiences saw her as a ray of hope and lapped up her movies. She grew up to be Ambassador to Ghana.

There were other child stars, of course. Deanna Durbin was terrifically popular singing her way through such films as *One Hundred Men and a Girl*, 1937. Never the cute little girl, she represented the appeal of adolescence seen

Seymour Felix won an Academy Award for the dance direction of this production number in *The Great Ziegfeld* (1936). *Inset :* William Powell as Florenz Ziegfeld and Myrna Loy as his wife; Billie Burke, in *The Great Ziegfeld*. The picture won the Academy Award as the best film of 1936. It was a mammoth musical drama for its time, running three hours, and recounting the life story of Broadway's great showman.

through rose-colored glasses. She was a hit in her first movie, *Three Smart Girls*, 1936, when she was 13. In a way she belongs to the operatic tradition of the musical, for she had a classically trained voice. Part of her attraction was that she really could sing.

MGM had one of the greatest stars ever. She just happened to be a child but she would never outgrow her gifts. When she appeared with a stunning cast in *The Wizard of Oz*, the Hollywood musical reached its zenith.

Adapted from the L Frank Baum novel of the same name, the movie quite literally did it all. Frank Morgan, Ray Bolger, Bert Lahr, Jack Haley, Billie Burke, Margaret Hamilton, Charley Grapewin, Clara Blandick and the midgets were marvelous. Harold Arlen and E Y Harburg's songs have passed into legend. The color was beautiful, the special effects never bettered.

Originally, the film was to star Shirley Temple. Had that been the case we would have had a very different sort of movie. And, had some of the MGM bosses got their way, 'Over The Rainbow' would have been cut. Let us thank our lucky stars that didn't happen. Where would we be without Judy, alias Dorothy Gale, singing out her dream of escape from Kansas? Is there any question that she deserved the special Academy Award she received for her performance?

It took 29 sound stages and 65 separate sets to make *The Wizard of Oz*. But then, MGM's 30s' musicals were very lavish. Besides the *Broadway Melody* spectaculars, they did *The Great Ziegfeld* with Myrna Loy playing Billie Burke, Ziegfeld's second wife, and William Powell as Ziegfeld. The pictorial follies knock your eye out. The film has everything from Pagliacci to revolving platforms, 'Rhapsody In Blue' by Gershwin and a $220,000 version of 'A Pretty Girl Is Like A Melody' so elaborate it's guaranteed to drive you to drink.

Where was Paramount while all this razzle-dazzle was going on at MGM? Paramount had 'Bing.' Harry Lillis Crosby had been catapulted into success by radio. He made a number of musicals in the 30s, mostly low-key mellow films, nothing lavish. One of the most interesting is *Pennies from Heaven*, 1936, remade by Steve Martin in 1981. It was a bit of a downer for Crosby but it has plenty of the Hollywood manna from heaven solution to depression woes.

Crosby made a number of movies with Martha Raye, including *Rhythm On The Range*, 1936 and *Double or Nothing*, 1937. But great things were ahead for Bing in the 40s, especially the 'Road' pictures with Dorothy Lamour and Bob Hope. The same could be said of Alice Faye, Judy Garland, Mickey Rooney, Betty Grable and a number of other stars who were around in the 30s yet whose names are invariably associated with the next era.

America marched out of the depression into World War II and the second great decade of the movie musical. Only this time it isn't all written in black and white. Glorious lip-smacking technicolor had arrived.

FOUR

In Glorious Technicolor

Remember that idol of the 30s, the platinum blond? We met her over and over again but whatever her name she always had the same silver hair, skin like Snow White, and a dress with sequins on it. She glimmered. This darling of the silver screen was a creation of black and white film. Technicolor gave her the boot.

With color we got variety. Blondes came in all shades and suddenly we noticed their eyes. Would Rita Hayworth have been a Love Goddess one decade sooner? Technicolor made redheads the rage.

Technicolor was strong and potent and about as realistic as a picture postcard. What it did for cosmetics! Crimson lipstick made Betty Grable's mouth kissable. Lana Turner's nails were like jewels. And costumes were sensational. Period musicals were big in the 40s partly because audiences got a chance to see yards and yards of vivid glowing fabrics. When you wore green, you wore green.

Color wasn't the only thing that happened to the musical. Arthur Freed was another. He was a film executive who first came to MGM at the time *The Wizard of Oz* was filmed. After that he made *Babes In Arms*, the first of the Mickey and Judy movies. Soon he had gathered his own group of top professionals. The Freed Unit was born. During the ensuing years it included Vincente Minnelli, Gene Kelly, Busby Berkeley, Red Skelton, Fred Astaire and Cyd Charisse among its luminaries. Script and song

Right : James Cagney played George M Cohan in *Yankee Doodle Dandy* (1942) and won the Academy Award that year as best actor. Behind him, left to right: Jeanne Cagney, Joan Leslie, Walter Huston and Rosemary DeCamp as the members of his family.
Opposite inset : Rooney and Garland teamed up for the first time in *Babes in Arms* (1939). It was based upon the 1937 Rodgers and Hart stage musical, but only two songs from the play were retained; one of them was 'Where or When.'

writers like Comden and Green, Cole Porter, Ira Gershwin, Johnny Mercer, and E Y Harburg were part of the Freed Unit. There would have been no *Cabin In The Sky*, *Meet Me In St Louis*, *On The Town*, *An American In Paris* or, most important of all, *Singin' In The Rain*, without Freed.

Picture number one, *Babes In Arms*, was based on the 1937 Rodgers and Hart stage show. Only two of the songs from the show were kept in the movie, however. MGM, like most studios, liked new songs. If one or two became hits the studios stood to make a lot of extra money.

Busby Berkeley was the director and the two whiz kids, Mickey Rooney and Judy Garland, were brought on the set to work their magic. They did. Teenagers have never been the same since.

When something works Hollywood generally works the formula again. So 1940 saw *Strike Up The Band*. The plot is as ever. Nice decent all-American kids are having a hard time through no fault of their own. 'Hey, kid, let's put on a show' shouted at the key moment means salvation is at hand. There is enough sentimentality to make you reach for your Kleenex and an awful lot of good singing on the screen. Judy's 'Do The Conga' is a joy.

Babes On Broadway, 1941, brings us the old plot again. This time when they say 'Hey, kids, let's do a show,' they mean in New York. Mickey does a Franklin Delano Roosevelt take-off. The true-blue teens sing their hearts out and it's on to *Girl Crazy*, 1943.

Above : Ethel Waters was the star of *Cabin in the Sky* (1942). It was an all-black musical drama, a variation on the Faust theme, and marked an important step forward in Hollywood's humanizing of black people.

Opposite top : *Babes on Broadway* (1941) was another 'Hey, kids, let's put on a show' effort from Mickey Rooney and Judy Garland. It was a showcase vehicle for them and they did everything from imitations of Carmen Miranda and Sarah Bernhardt to minstrel numbers. The standout number was Judy's 'Franklin D Roosevelt Jones.'

Opposite bottom : A publicity shot for *Girl Crazy* (1943). Mickey, Judy and Tommy Dorsey being checked out by a group of chorus cowgirls.

This time Mickey isn't a complete goody-goody. He chases girls. So Mickey is banished to the West by a disapproving father. He attends Cody College, which is on the verge of financial collapse. There, he falls in love with the dean's granddaughter—Judy, of course. Mickey saves the college by coming up with his usual cure for the economic blues: 'Kids, let's. . .' They do. The gang puts on a musical rodeo. Judy and Mickey dance. Money is raised. Everything's super. And that was that. No more Mickey and Judy musicals. Still, no matter how repetitious the plot, how insane the story line, the movies had style and are fun to watch even now. And they did feature two legendary talents in an important phase of their careers.

But the Mickey-Judy movies, simple, straightforward, with a focus on character, were just one side of the MGM musical coin. MGM still produced extravaganzas. *Ziegfeld Girl* appeared in 1941. A biggie, it was definitely a hybrid, part 30s, part 40s film. Produced by Freed, directed by Minnelli and with a crowd of other leading talents, it seemed to star the entire MGM studio. Fred Astaire, Lucille Ball, Judy Garland, Lena Horne, Gene Kelly, Red Skelton, Esther Williams, Cyd Charisse and Louis Bunin's Puppets, to name a few. Filmed in black and white it has a formula plot in the 'Kid, you'll be a big star on Broadway' tradition. It has a certain galumphing zest and seemingly endless cameo appearances. In the number 'You Stepped Out of A Dream' Hedy Lamarr and Lana Turner strut their stuff.

In 1938 20th Century-Fox had made *Alexander's Ragtime Band* with Alice Faye, Don Ameche, Tyrone Power, Ethel Merman and Jack Haley. Its popularity was based partly on a nostalgic view of America's past. This nostalgia was to thunder across America during and after World War II. But, to a lesser extent, Hollywood was having a love affair with another part of the continent and from the 30s through a good chunk of the 40s, musicals were made with a Latin motif.

Down Argentine Way came out in 1940. It should have starred Alice Faye. She couldn't make it. The girl who got the lead was Betty Grable. It was the big break she needed. There is another first for the film. Carmen Miranda, with fruit on her head and fire in her eye, made her debut in pictures.

She was so small she wore six inch heels. She was a well-known singer in Brazil before she ever reached Hollywood. Just as America demanded that its black performers behave in certain stereotyped ways—dumb, sexy, lazy—so all South Americans were supposed to be passionate, violent, and spoiled by living in a warm climate. Carmen Miranda's campy accent and style made her a natural for the part of hot jealous senhorita.

This doesn't mean she wasn't any good. The racism of the time also devalued the artistry of Lena Horne, Ethel Waters and Bill Robinson. Whatever the image, Carmen Miranda sang with gusto and had a comic flair. She was enormously assisted by technicolor, which showed off her wild costumes and headdresses to the fullest.

Busby Berkeley, who had an eye for the exotic, used her to perfection in *The Gang's All Here*, 1943, when she wore a banana hat thirty feet high! Surrounded by giant strawberries her hat extends to an infinity even Einstein couldn't imagine. It got knocked off during filming and caused a panic.

Another name associated with the Hollywood urge for Spanish culture is José Iturbi. Born in Spain, he was an actor, musician and conductor. Xavier Cugat also made it big in the movies. Alice Faye finally got her day in the sun in *That Night In Rio*, 1941, and *Weekend In Havana*, the same year.

The most important man in the story of the musical with a Latin beat is none other than Walt Disney. Wonderful Walt had completed a number of cartoon masterpieces. Though they have music they do not belong to the musical genre. *Snow White* and *Fantasia* are something else.

With war raging across Europe in the 1940s, South America looked good. Besides, Disney was seeking new markets to make up for the European loss. That, coupled with a natural attraction to what lay just across the border from California, got Disney going.

He made a travelogue cum cartoon called *Saludos Amigos*. We meet the Disney staff, see Donald Duck play a tourist, and are introduced to a new and important character, a bird named Joe Carioca whose voice belonged to José Oliveira in real life. Later Walt brought us *The Three Caballeros*, released by RKO pictures in 1945.

Opposite top : Alice Faye sings to the accompaniment of Tyrone Power and his orchestra in *Alexander's Ragtime Band* (1938). Jack Haley plays the drums while Don Ameche pounds the piano. This was a large-scale musical with many fine Irving Berlin songs—'Now It Can Be Told,' 'My Walking Stick' and 'I'm Marching Along With Time' among them.
Opposite bottom : In *Down Argentine Way* (1940), Betty Grable and Don Ameche recoil from J Carrol Naish. Alice Faye had been signed for the film and couldn't make it, so this was Grable's big chance.
Top : Carmen Miranda, who stole the show in *That Night in Rio* (1941).
Above : The romantic pair in *That Night in Rio*—Don Ameche and Alice Faye.

We can safely say this important film is a musical because though there is animation, there are live people too. The color is beautiful, the songs are fun, and the image of a cheerful sun-drenched South America permeated the public's consciousness. It became the image of the lands to our south for some years. We can see a more realistic assessment by the time of *West Side Story*, but in the 1940s it was Disney, Carmen Miranda and the samba.

Disney went on to make other films with live people and animated characters, eventually giving us pictures without any animation at all. *Song of the South* with James Baskett as Uncle Remus is one of the best musicals. There's *Melody Time*, 1948, and *So Dear To My Heart*, same year. And, of course, in 1964 came one of the most important musicals of all time, *Mary Poppins*, with Julie Andrews as the prim and magical Miss Poppins and Dick Van Dyke as her chimney sweep of a boyfriend. No history of the musical would be complete without the one and only Walt Disney.

With the boys in uniform scattered around the globe, Hollywood did its best to keep up morale with a series of straight propaganda films and musical propaganda films. The musicals, of course, didn't beat you over the head with tales of Axis horrors. Instead, they reminded you what you were fighting for.

Paramount released *Star-Spangled Rhythm* in 1942. Paulette Goddard, Dorothy Lamour and Veronica Lake sang 'A Sweater, A Sarong and a Peek-a-boo Bang.' Warners brought out *Thank Your Lucky Stars* with Bette Davis's rendition of 'They're Either Too Young Or Too Old.' MGM had *Thousands Cheer* in 1943, culminating in 'United Nations Salute,' a boost for the Allies; 1944 witnessed *Music For Millions* with Jimmy Durante.

During the war Hollywood, like everybody else, had to contend with shortages. Some of its top stars were either in the service or off entertaining the troops. But there were some awfully good movies nonetheless. Take *Anchors Aweigh*, MGM, 1945. This was Gene Kelly's first true lead at MGM. He played a sailor, and would play servicemen for a long time to come. But, then, everybody was a sailor or soldier in movies that year. Gene's talent and appeal were evident from the start. He was on his way to becoming a major star.

Paramount's *The Fleet's In* was an earlier film in 1942. It featured the great comedy and musical performer Betty Hutton and the funny Mr Eddie Bracken.

Columbia's *You'll Never Get Rich*, 1941, had Fred Astaire dancing with a beautiful up-and-coming starlet named Rita Hayworth, which brings us to an important fact about 40s films. The dames, as they would have said in those days, were real tomatoes. Maybe it was the boys on the battlefields craving pinups. Maybe it was, as said earlier, the luscious effects of technicolor. Whatever it was, when you think of the 30s, the male stars of musicals stand out in your mind. But, with a few exceptions, the big names in the 40s' musicals were women.

Twentieth Century's gift to the war effort was Betty

Above left : Brer Rabbit in Walt Disney's *Song of the South* (1946). The film recounted some of the Joel Chandler Harris 'Uncle Remus' stories and combined animation with real actors.

Top : Left to right: the extremely talented child star, Margaret O'Brien, Marsha Hunt and Jimmy Durante in *Music for Millions* (1944), a teary tale of sisters joining José Iturbi's orchestra. Durante stole the show with 'Umbriago.'

Above : Eddie Bracken and Betty Hutton in *The Fleet's In* (1942). Some of the songs from the film were 'Tangerine,' 'I Remember You' and 'The Fleet's In.' Also starring were Dorothy Lamour and William Holden.

Left : Julie Andrews and Dick Van Dyke were the stars of *Mary Poppins* (1964), possibly Walt Disney's most successful movie. It was a fantasy based upon the works of P L Travers about a magical nanny who descends on a family in Edwardian London.

Grable. Like her glorious predecessor of the previous decade, the immortal Marlene Dietrich, she was a sex symbol famous for her legs. You could see her picture in Europe, in the South Pacific, anywhere the war was. The boys saw to that.

For about 10 years she was a superstar like few before or since. Dan Dailey, Don Ameche, John Payne, Victor Mature and Dick Haymes were her co-stars. When she married the great musician, Harry James, it made news.

Like many a star, Betty was lucky enough to be in the right place at the right time for her particular gifts. She had a beaming toothpaste ad smile which came across in color. She wasn't so beautiful or so exotic that you worshipped her from afar. Rather she had a bland amiability. She was a good-looking but basically ordinary girl that GI Joe might meet in a small town diner or find working in a war plant in a big city. She was nice. You felt you had a chance if you could just get to know her. Well, a boy can dream, can't he? Betty Grable got ten thousand or more fan letters a week at the height of her career!

In 1944 she made, appropriately, *Pin Up Girl.* In 1945 Billy Rose's *Diamond Horseshoe* hit the screens of America. The pretty girls who smiled their way through in the background actually appeared in one scene wearing desserts on their hats. Ah, Hollywood!

With the war came jobs and the breadlines vanished, so it was no longer necessary to escape into a world of the rich. Europe, overrun by Hitler's troops, didn't seem a very good place to set anything as frothy as a musical. The USA turned inward and the public clamored for movies set in a prosperous happy American past. Values that stressed home and family emerged in musicals, ousting the snappy irreverence of the 30s.

So Grable made *Coney Island* in 1943. If you believed this movie, there was no litter in Coney Island at the turn of the century and saloon keepers had the morals of ministers.

1945 brought us *The Dolly Sisters* with Grable and June Haver. This time the chorus girls don't look like Baked Alaska. No, this time around they were cast as lipstick, rouge and, to single one chorine out, Patsy Powder Puff. After the war, the nostalgic mood still held sway and Betty Grable made one of her best musicals, *Mother Wore Tights* in 1947. *When My Baby Smiles At Me* a year later introduced a more serious note, as she played the wife of a vaudeville comedian who drinks. *Wabash Avenue* and *Call Me Mister* followed but her movie career was drawing to a close.

In 1944 *Cover Girl* was released. It put Rita Hayworth up there in the glittering Hollywood firmament. She was a striking beauty with enormous sex appeal and there is no need to puzzle over the origin of her attractiveness. Born Margarita Carmen Cansino, she was originally a dancer. Besides being a movie star she became an international cafe society figure. At one time she was married to Orson Welles, the noted actor. Later, she married Ali Khan, one of the world's richest playboys.

Samuel Goldwyn's *Up In Arms* in 1944 introduced one

of the more endearing performers of our time, Danny Kaye. Playing opposite chiefly Virginia Mayo or Vera-Ellen he made a string of movies which are primarily comedies but which have strong musical moments.

Bing Crosby was still crooning his way through the movies. In 1942 he appeared with Fred Astaire in *Holiday Inn*, a low-key pleasant musical with the mellow glow of wartime values. The home front certainly looked worth coming home to. Two other big stars, Lucille Ball and Red Skelton, made *Du Barry Was A Lady* and Ginger Rogers appeared in the sophisticated *Lady In the Dark*. *Best Foot Forward*, 1943, showcased the talents of three rising young starlets, June Allyson, Gloria De Haven, and Nancy Walker.

Esther Williams, a champion athlete at 15, was taken up by MGM which needed its own version of 20th Century-Fox's Sonja Henie. Besides looking very nice, if a bit broad-shouldered, in the classic one-piece bathing suit of the day, Esther added a new dimension to the Hollywood extravaganza: water. Starting with *Bathing Beauty*, 1944,

Top: In this scene from *Cover Girl* (1944), Gene Kelly, Rita Hayworth and Phil Silvers eat at a luncheonette. The counterman is Edward S Brophy. This was the film that put Hayworth in the motion-picture star firmament.
Above: Red Skelton (center) and Lucille Ball in *Du Barry Was a Lady* (1943). The Cole Porter score for the film included 'Do I Love You, Do I?,' 'Friendship' and 'Katie Went to Haiti.'

she went on to make a number of movies including *On An Island With You*, 1948, and *Neptune's Daughter*, 1949. She didn't so much play opposite as swim opposite leading men such as Howard Keel and Ricardo Montalban. Miss Piggy does a wonderful spoof of an aquatic ballet in *The Great Muppet Caper*.

One of the best of the 40s musicals was *Cabin In The Sky*. With a plot reminiscent of the later all-white *Damn Yankees* its black cast included Ethel Waters and Lena Horne. The songs by Harold Arlen and 'Yip' Harburg featured 'Happiness Is Just A Thing Called Joe' and 'Taking A Chance On Love.'

Movies about composers went down big in the 40s. Although the composers' lives were sanitized and sentimentalized, the films provided audiences with an opportunity to hear a lot of good music. Most notable was James Cagney as a bouncy George M Cohan in *Yankee Doodle Dandy*. *Rhapsody In Blue* starred Robert Alda as George Gershwin and Oscar Levant as Oscar Levant. Cary Grant was Cole Porter in *Night and Day*. *The Jolson Story* with Larry Parks followed the formula and was so successful it revived Jolson's career.

Having outgrown the Mickey-Judy format, the wondrous Garland went on to make some of her greatest films in the 40s. In 1944 *Meet Me In St Louis* was released. With the assistance of Margaret O'Brien, who was to be the child star of the decade, and a superb cast, Judy sang her way into the hearts of the American Heartland. Though it cloys a bit now, the movie is a masterpiece of craftsmanship. It was made with love and care and it shows.

The Harvey Girls, MGM, 1946, is another historical musical epic. Judy's rival is a no-good little low-down saloon girl played by Angela Lansbury who was all of 19 at the time. The movie's big song is 'On the Atchison, Topeka and the Santa Fe.'

Not everything was done in historical garb, however. The 40s witnessed a series of college 'rah, rah, let's have fun' musicals, for example, a remake of *Good News* with Peter Lawford and June Allyson. Jane Powell was singing her way through some light charming films, all in modern clothes.

But the real news of the 40s was being made by one Gene Kelly. When he and Vera-Ellen danced 'Slaughter On Tenth Avenue' in *Words and Music*, MGM, 1948, they made history. *On The Town*, a year later, is one of the best musicals ever. Filmed in part on location in New York, the choreography is super. Besides Kelly, Frank Sinatra, Jules Munshin, Vera-Ellen as the lovely 'Miss Turnstiles' and the dynamic Ann Miller deserve praise. The play within a play, 'A Day In New York,' shows Kelly's choreographic genius.

There will never again be a period of musical abundance like the 40s. Taken together the two decades of the 30s and 40s represent the golden age of the musical art form.

Hollywood has never quite been so totally Hollywood since.

Top: June Allyson and Peter Lawford doing 'The Varsity Drag' number from *Good News* (1948).
Above: *On the Town* (1949) was a huge success because of the music by Leonard Bernstein and the choreography by Jerome Robbins. The film told of a group of three sailors in New York on a 24-hour leave. Left to right: Betty Garrett, Ann Miller, Gene Kelly, Jules Munshin, Frank Sinatra, Alice Pearce.
Opposite top: *The Jolson Story* was the film biography of the popular singer, starting with his boyhood and ending with his success on the stage and in films. It starred Larry Parks, but the voice was dubbed by Jolson himself.
Opposite bottom: It has been said that her role in *Meet Me in St Louis* (1944) was the best in Judy Garland's career. Here Judy and young Margaret O'Brien entertain their brother and sisters.

FIVE

Little Nifties From the Fifties

s there life after the 40s? The answer is a resounding yes. Although the prolific era of the musical was over, some of the most cherished movies appeared in the decade that brought you television. And television was filmdom's lion-sized competitor.

Not all the films were innovative. Mario Lanza and Kathryn Grayson had made *That Midnight Kiss* in 1949, a movie that Jeanette MacDonald and Nelson Eddy would have felt at home in. The pair are together again in 1950 for a rematch, *The Toast Of New Orleans*. Period costumes and lots of arias did it for this one. Lanza made one of the biggest pictures of the year in 1951, *The Great Caruso*, with Ann Blyth as Mrs Caruso. Lanza continued to make films afterwards, but he was on a downward spiral emotionally and physically and he died young.

The hero of the 50s musical is Gene Kelly. *On The Town* was not merely clever. It has the look and feel of a new era. Kelly had learned his trade well. From the time he first worked with Busby Berkeley, he became fascinated with what the camera does. The shots of the real New York in *On The Town* give audiences a vista of freedom no cardboard backdrop could convey.

In the 50s the Freed Unit at MGM flourished. There was *Annie Get Your Gun* with the human dynamo Betty Hutton in her finest film. *Royal Wedding* came next with Fred Astaire. Fred had quit the screen for a while but he

Right : The King and I (1956) starred Yul Brynner as the king of Siam and Deborah Kerr as Anna Leonowens, the teacher of his many children. The plot of the 1948 film *Anna and the King of Siam* was adapted by Rodgers and Hammerstein, who added such songs as 'Getting to Know You,' 'I Whistle a Happy Tune,' 'Hello, Young Lovers' and 'Shall We Dance?' Kerr's singing voice was dubbed by Marni Nixon.

returned to make several films which fueled his legend. Even though his dancing was not what it had been 20 years earlier (20 years!) his imaginative choreography won the day.

In 1951 MGM created a landmark in movie history, *An American In Paris*. Leslie Caron was a very shy young French dancer, pretty in an unconventional way. She was a risk for the studio, but so was a planned 17 minute ballet. Tap and chorus lines were supposed to dominate musicals. Excluding *The Red Shoes* it was unheard of to have a super-long dance sequence without song or dialogue to keep the audience awake.

The movie was a smash, beating out *A Streetcar Named Desire* for Academy Award-winning Best Picture of the Year. Kelly won an Oscar, too. That was March, 1952. A better movie lay ahead. The best, in fact.

1952 saw *Singin' In The Rain*. Occasionally everything goes right. A young kid still in her teens named Debbie Reynolds had caught the public fancy singing 'Aba Daba Honeymoon' with Carleton Carpenter in the movie *Two Weeks With Love*, 1950. She got the female lead. Donald O'Connor was around to do some of the best comic dancing ever. Comden and Green were at their wittiest. Kelly was there. The result? A gentle spoof with the best singing, best dancing ever, including the most famous scene from any musical, Gene Kelly wetly singing and dancing the title song. The picture went way over budget and was worth every penny.

Top: Leslie Caron and Gene Kelly in *An American in Paris* (1951). This Academy Award-winning film boasted a book by Alan Jay Lerner with a George and Ira Gershwin score, plus Kelly's choreography and Vincente Minnelli's direction.

Above: Singin' in the Rain (1952) made a star of Debbie Reynolds, shown here between Gene Kelly and Donald O'Connor.

In 1954 one of *Singin' In The Rain*'s directors, Stanley Donen, produced another masterpiece. *Seven Brides For Seven Brothers* was a throwback to the nostalgic period piece film of the 40s, when Americana was the rage. It stars Howard Keel, Jane Powell and Russ Tamblyn. The Gene de Paul-Johnny Mercer songs are good. The dancing is terrific and the whole film, based very very roughly on the story of the rape of the Sabine women, is a buoyant tribute to the art of the movie musical.

The Band Wagon in 1953, again with a great script by Betty Comden and Adolph Green, shows off the talents of Fred Astaire, Nanette Fabray and the beautiful dancer, Cyd Charisse, who may be able to lay claim to having the longest legs in the world. 'The Girl Hunt,' the show within the show, is a very neat little satire of Mickey Spillane's mysteries.

The same year audiences flocked to see Leslie Caron's best movie, *Lili*. This is as much a fantasy as a musical, with its gentle puppeteer Mel Ferrer, its carnival setting and its sweet fairy tale love story.

Busby Berkeley, still up to his old tricks, put Ann Miller through her paces in *Small Town Girl*, MGM, 1953, which starred Jane Powell. Bing Crosby, durable as ever, made *White Christmas* in 1954. This time he had Danny Kaye, Rosemary Clooney and Vera-Ellen, still spunky, starring with him.

The great Fred Astaire had another triumph when he was paired with one of the most delightful stars of the 50s,

Top : The barn raising ballet from *Seven Brides for Seven Brothers* (1954). Based loosely on a short story by Stephen Vincent Benét, this tune-filled yarn tells of six fur-trapping brothers who come to town to find wives.
Above : After the eldest brother (Howard Keel) has married Jane Powell, that left six brides in *Seven Brides for Seven Brothers.*

Audrey Hepburn. Together they made *Funny Face*, Paramount, 1957. Leslie Caron had another triumph, too. *Gigi*, in 1958, placed her opposite the handsome Louis Jourdan. Another period piece, this time with a French accent all the way around, the movie is based on the sparkling Colette story.

Although musicals tapered off over the decade, a pert blond named Doris Day rode them right to the top. *On Moonlight Bay*, 1951, and *By The Light of the Silvery Moon*, 1953, were popular but her best movie was *Pajama Game*, 1957. This Warner Brothers film choreographed by Bob Fosse with its story about a union in a pajama factory is a charmer. Carol Haney's 'Steam Heat' is one of the high spots.

There weren't many original Hollywood musicals being made anymore. Practically all the big releases were based on Broadway shows. But there was a young man named Elvis Presley who did a series of popular films that were completely his own, for example, *Jailhouse Rock*, made by MGM in 1957.

Above : The Pajama Game (1957) starred John Raitt and Doris Day. The plot revolved around a pajama factory union's efforts to get a seven-and-one-half-cent hourly increase. Raitt played the factory manager and Day was a union leader. The hit song was 'Hey There.'
Opposite top left : Leslie Caron and Mel Ferrer starred in *Lili* (1953), the musical about a French orphan girl who joins a carnival and attaches herself to a self-pitying puppeteer. The song, 'Hi Lili Hi Lo' won an Oscar.
Opposite top right : Funny Face (1957) starred Fred Astaire and Audrey Hepburn. It was a musical about a fashion photographer who turns a girl working in a bookshop into a high-fashion model, and had top Gershwin tunes.
Opposite bottom : Leslie Caron continued to play an innocent French girl in *Gigi* (1958). Also in the cast were Maurice Chevalier (standing, left), Hermione Gingold and Louis Jourdan. The score was by Lerner and Loewe and contained such hits as 'Gigi' and 'Thank Heaven for Little Girls.'

Above: Gene Kelly and Van Johnson starred in *Brigadoon* (1954). Here they are being pursued by Eddie Quillan. The film was the story of a Scottish village that came to life every hundred years for one day only, and contained such Allan Jay Lerner-Frederick Loewe songs as 'The Heather on the Hill,' 'Almost Like Being In Love,' 'There But for You Go I' and 'Brigadoon.'

Opposite: It's rare that two authentic screen goddesses appear in the same film, but here are Jane Russell and Marilyn Monroe as seen in *Gentlemen Prefer Blondes* (1953). It was an updated screen version of the Broadway play about two show business beauties on the prowl on a boat taking them to France. The hit song? 'Diamonds Are a Girl's Best Friend.'

In 1951 Hollywood had brought *Show Boat* to the screen, with Kathryn Grayson and Howard Keel. Not only was this the remake of a stage show, it was a remake of an earlier film. In 1936 *Show Boat* had starred Irene Dunne and Allan Jones. As the 50s wore on, Hollywood began basing its films on more recent Broadway hits.

Kismet and *Brigadoon* came to the movies. *Kiss Me Kate* made its romping way across the big screen of the 1950s. MGM's *Silk Stockings* was based on *Ninotchka*, Garbo's comic glory. In its musical format it starred Fred Astaire and Cyd Charisse. *Gentlemen Prefer Blondes*, 1953, gave us the opportunity to observe several ample bosoms in action, especially Jane Russell's and Marilyn Monroe's. *Call Me Madam*, 1953, gave us pure gold, the incomparable Ethel Merman.

Top: Gordon MacRae and Shirley Jones were the leads in Rodgers and Hammerstein's Musical *Carousel* (1956), a tastefully produced adaptation of their Broadway hit, which was based on the Ferenc Molnar play *Liliom*. It concerns the marriage of a swaggering carnival barker and a shy girl, and the tragic consequences when he takes drastic steps to provide for their child. Some of the songs from the film were 'If I Loved You,' 'You'll Never Walk Alone' and 'June Is Bustin' Out All Over.'
Above: The 'June Is Bustin' Out All Over' ballet from *Carousel*.

Rodgers and Hammerstein's music was everywhere. *Carousel*, 1956, featured the lovely Shirley Jones and Gordon MacRae in one of the all-time tear jerkers. *The King And I*, 1956, is a lavish spectacular which, of course, stars Yul Brynner as the king and Deborah Kerr as Anna. She wears the fullest skirts in history.

Oklahoma! was a 1955 hit. Filmed in wide-screen Todd-AO, it was based on the stage show which had transformed the Broadway musical 12 years earlier.

South Pacific arrived in 1958, with Rossano Brazzi and Mitzi Gaynor. Hollywood was coming full circle, worshipping Broadway shows and Broadway stars as it hadn't since talkies began.

1958 saw *Damn Yankees* with the delicious Gwen Verdon. *Pal Joey*, 1957, with Frank Sinatra, is nowhere near as cynical as its Broadway predecessor. The 1955 *Guys and Dolls*, produced by Samuel Goldwyn, offered up Marlon Brando as the honorable gambler, Sky Masterson, and Frank Sinatra as Nathan Detroit. With its talented supporting cast and good music it's one of the best musicals of the 50s.

Above : South Pacific (1958) was another adaptation of a Rodgers and Hammerstein Broadway musical, and was about the romance between a US Army nurse and a suave French planter on an island in the South Pacific during World War II. It featured such songs as 'Some Enchanted Evening,' 'There Is Nothing Like a Dame,' 'Bali H'ai,' 'You've Got to Be Taught' and 'This Nearly Was Mine.' Here Mitzi Gaynor as Nellie Forbush, the nurse, entertains the sailors with her 'Honey Bun' routine.

Opposite below right : Oklahoma! (1955) was a hit. It was the first picture filmed in wide-screen Todd-AO and was based upon the Rodgers and Hammerstein Broadway musical that had changed the look of the musical comedy 12 years before. Here, Gene Nelson does his 'Everything's Up to Date in Kansas City' song-and-dance number.

In 1959 George Gershwin's *Porgy and Bess* starred Dorothy Dandridge and Sidney Poitier, both with their singing voices dubbed. Pearl Bailey and Sammy Davis Jr add life. Unfortunately, the 50s Hollywood musical was beginning to creak. Frequently overlong, it relied too much on dubbed performances, on stars who didn't know their left foot from their right. The sparkle, ingenuity, and authenticity were starting to go.

There are exceptions. Judy Garland rises to glorious new heights in *A Star Is Born,* Warner's 1954 remake of an earlier film. *High Society* with Bing Crosby, Grace Kelly, and Frank Sinatra has its flaws but is a classy musical. Films like *The Glenn Miller Story*, Universal, 1954, with Jimmy Stewart and June Allyson, gave people old-fashioned pleasure.

But audiences were home watching variety shows on television now rather than movie musicals. Though there were still some big block-busters left and stars would be made in the musicals of the following decade, the bloom was off the rose in Hollywood.

Left : Gwenn Verdon tried to seduce Tab Hunter in the 'Whatever Lola Wants' sequence in *Damn Yankees* (1958). This was one of the few films with a sports theme to make it big.
Below : In the crap game scene from *Guys and Dolls* (1955), Marlon Brando sings 'Luck Be a Lady.' Other Frank Loesser songs were 'A Woman in Love' and 'If I Were a Bell.'
Opposite : Porgy and Bess (1959) was the film version of the George Gershwin opera and starred Sidney Poitier and Dorothy Dandridge in the title roles.

SIX

The Sun Sinks Slowly Over the West

It cost a lot of money to make a musical in the 60s. So not very many were made. The wide screen presented technical difficulties which didn't help matters any. But there were a few silk purses among the sows' ears and we can stroll happily along our visual Memory Lane.

The Music Man, 1962, with Robert Preston and Shirley Jones, is a happy summer day kind of thing. Billy Rose's *Jumbo* took us to the circus. *Gypsy*, 1962, presents the story of Gypsy Rose Lee and her sister June Havoc. Rosalind Russell makes a great stage mama and Natalie Wood is darling and even touching as her daughter Louise.

Funny Girl, 1968, let film audiences get to know Barbra Streisand, one of the big musical makers of our time and a star in the style of the old superstar of Hollywood's earlier more glorious days. *Hello, Dolly*, 1969, has her singing a fabulous duet with Louis Armstrong.

Judy Holliday, the talented comedian whose early death ended a notable career, appeared in one musical just as the decade rolled in, *Bells Are Ringing*, MGM. *Flower Drum Song*, 1961, gave us Jack Soo in the Rodgers and Hammerstein musical set in San Francisco's Chinatown. *How To Succeed In Business Without Really Trying*, 1967, is cheery and *Sweet Charity*, Universal, 1969, has Shirley MacLaine.

Among the top gems of the decade are *West Side Story*, 1961. There's good dancing and top talent Rita Moreno.

Right : A dance number from *Hello, Dolly!* (1969), the musical version of Thornton Wilder's play *The Matchmaker*.
Opposite inset : John Travolta, fresh from his *Saturday Night Fever* hit, leads his grease monkeys in a dance number in *Grease* (1978). It was a film adaptation of the musical that ran on Broadway longer than any musical comedy with the exception of *A Chorus Line*.

Above : Robert Preston, as Professor Harold Hill, leads his 'Seventy-Six Trombones' in *The Music Man.*
Left : Left to right: Natalie Wood, Rosalind Russell and Karl Malden sing the 'Together' number in *Gypsy* (1962). The score by Jule Styne and Stephen Sondheim boasted such songs as 'Everything's Coming up Roses' and 'Let Me Entertain You.'

Above : Left to right: Franco Nero as Lancelot, Richard Harris as King Arthur and Vanessa Redgrave as Guenevere in *Camelot* (1967).
Left : Audrey Hepburn is dressed to leave for the Ascot races as Rex Harrison looks on dubiously in *My Fair Lady* (1964). They starred as Eliza Doolittle and Professor Henry Higgins in the Lerner and Loewe adaptation of George Bernard Shaw's *Pygmalion.* Marni Nixon did the dubbing for Hepburn's singing voice and Harrison won an Oscar for his role as the British gentleman who turns a Cockney flower girl into a lady.
Below : A publicity still for *Fiddler on the Roof* (1971), the the story of a group of Jewish peasants in the Ukraine in 1905, taken from the writings of Sholem Aleichem. The Sheldon Harnick-Jerry Bock score contained such songs as 'If I Were a Rich Man,' 'Tevye's Dream' and 'Matchmaker.' The rooftop violin solo of 'Fiddler on the Roof' was played by Isaac Stern.

My Fair Lady pairs the by now top star Audrey Hepburn with Rex Harrison for another reworking of the G B Shaw work of art, *Pygmalion.*

Camelot, 1967, looks expensive but drags. *Oliver,* 1968, brings us Fagin's old gang, prettied up for the kids' crowd. Julie Andrews, whose lovely voice and winning personality made her a leader of the 60s songsters, made *The Sound of Music,* 20th Century-Fox, 1965.

Two of the best musicals of the 60s starred an English singing group called The Beatles: *A Hard Day's Night* and *Help!*

By the 1970s the lights were dimming. We have *Mame,* Warner's excuse to star Lucille Ball, who had triumphed on television, *Fiddler On The Roof,* a too reverent version of the enormous Broadway hit, and at last something to crow about, *Cabaret.*

Liza Minnelli won an Oscar for her role in this musical variation of the Christopher Isherwood Berlin Stories. Joel Grey turns in an unforgettable performance, embodying the decadence of Germany during the early 30s. Liza, the daughter of Judy Garland, made her debut in 1949, when her mother played opposite Van Johnson. The film was *In The Good Old Summertime.*

The Wiz came in 1978, a black version of The Wizard of Oz. Stunning in its costumes, the movie failed despite having a lot of talent in the form of Diana Ross, Michael Jackson and Richard Pryor as the Wiz himself.

John Travolta, fresh from his Saturday Night Fever hit, made Grease in 1978. Eulogizing the 50s, it did very well indeed at the box office. Hair, eulogizing the 60s, did not. We have had Grease II but not Hair II. All That Jazz, 1979, is a dazzling example of Bob Fosse's versatility. The Rose, with Bette Midler, though not precisely a musical, is one of a long tradition of movies with music about musical stars. In a more sentimental age Susan Hayward excelled at that sort of thing. She played Jane Froman in With A Song in My Heart, 1952 and I'll Cry Tomorrow, 1955, a film biography of Lillian Roth. The Buddy Holly Story, Columbia, 1978, with Gary Busey, is a more recent representative of the genre.

The Jazz Singer, remade for the third (no less) time, Pennies From Heaven, a spoof with Steve Martin, and the little orphan girl who takes New York by storm, Annie, prove that Hollywood still has the old spark. A Chorus Line is next.

Though the tapping shoes are now merely an echo, and the silver screen shines no more, we have our memories. Great ones.

So, favorite shows, you're ours still. We'll see you in our dreams.

Top : The crucifixion scene from *Jesus Christ, Superstar* (1973). Filmed in Israel, the movie told the story of the Passion. Its most popular song was 'I Don't Know How to Love Him,' as sung by Mary Magdalene.
Above : Beverly D'Angelo and John Savage getting married in *Hair* (1979).
Opposite : Liza Minnelli won the Academy Award for best actress for *Cabaret* (1972). The film presented a vivid picture of the seamy side of Berlin life in the early 1930s and won a total of seven Oscars.

SEVEN

The Stars

Ameche, Don (1908–)

Leading man in many Fox musicals of the 30s and 40s including *Alexander's Ragtime Band* and *Moon Over Miami*. Probably best known for his nonmusical title role in *Alexander Graham Bell*.

Andrews, Julie (1935–)

Born Julia Wells in Britain, she became a major Broadway star in *My Fair Lady*. She was passed over for the film version of the show, but she was the leading lady in two of the most successful film musicals of all times, *Mary Poppins* and *The Sound of Music*. Recently has concentrated more on dramatic and comic roles.

Astaire, Fred (1899–)

Born Frederick Austerlitz, he came to the screen after having established a reputation as a dancer on stage in partnership with his sister, Adele. The studio report on his first screen test was 'Can't act. Can't sing. Can dance a little.' Studio reports notwithstanding Astaire was soon established as the screen's top song and dance man, a position he held for nearly 20 years, though he did not even make his first movie until he was over 30. He danced with many of the leading ladies of musicals during the 30s and 40s, but it was his partnership with Ginger Rogers in such films as *Top Hat* and *Swing Time*

Right : Cyd Charisse and Fred Astaire joined forces in *Silk Stockings* (1957). It was a musical remake of Greta Garbo's *Ninotchka* (1939) and the songs were Cole Porter's.
Opposite inset : Another Garland (here with Angela Lansbury) triumph was *The Harvey Girls* (1945). Among the songs in the Mercer-Warren score was 'On the Atchison, Topeka and the Santa Fe.'

Above : Footlight Parade (1933) was another in the Powell-Keeler Broadway mold, but it was important in that it gave James Cagney his first singing and dancing role in films. Here he dances on a table top with Keeler.
Below : Bing Crosby's second film was *The Big Broadcast* (1932). It was a light-hearted entertainment that used a zany story about a radio station to bring in many of the stars of the day.

that produced a special magic which makes those films every bit as entertaining today as they were when first made. Astaire has continued to appear in films in nondancing dramatic roles.

Bolger, Ray (1904–   )

American dancer, singer and comic who appeared in many musicals including *Stage Door Canteen* and *The Harvey Girls* but will always be remembered for his part as the Scarecrow in *The Wizard of Oz*.

Cagney, James (1899–   )

Began as a Broadway chorus boy, but became famous on the screen for his gangster parts. He did appear in some musicals; the best known was *Yankee Doodle Dandy* in which he played George M Cohan.

Cantor, Eddy (1892–1964)

Born Isidore Itzkowitz, he was a sprightly pop-eyed vaudeville comic and song and dance man. He was an established Broadway star before coming to Hollywood to make such films as *Whoopee, Roman Scandals* and *Thank Your Lucky Stars*. He was a huge hit on radio and *The Eddie Cantor Story* is his screen biography. Keefe Braselle played Cantor, but Cantor dubbed all the songs.

Caron, Leslie (1931–   )

French ballet dancer spotted by Gene Kelly in Paris. He recommended her for the female lead in *American In Paris*. She also appeared in several other major musicals—*Lili, Daddy Long Legs* and *Gigi*.

Charisse, Cyd (1921–   )

Born Tula Ellice Finklea, she began her career as a dancer with the Ballet Russe. She started in movie musicals in 1944 and did a long specialty number with Gene Kelly in *Singin' In The Rain*. She had starring roles in *The Band Wagon, Brigadoon* and *Silk Stockings*. Her singing was usually dubbed.

Chevalier, Maurice (1888–1972)

French cabaret and music hall star, whose symbols were a rakishly tilted straw hat and a jutting lower lip. He didn't start making films until he was over 40, but quickly became one of the most popular musical stars, with such films as *The Love Parade, Love Me Tonight* and *The Merry Widow*. Though his popularity declined, particularly during the years of World War II, when he was suspected—incorrectly—of being a Nazi collaborator, he was still a major star in the late 1950s when he made *Gigi* and *Can-Can*.

Crosby, Bing (1903–1977)

One of the most durable of American singers. He made his screen debut as a singer with the Paul Whiteman

orchestra in the 1930s, and then he developed into a star in his own right. His 'Road' pictures made with comedian Bob Hope, while not really musicals, always featured a few Crosby songs. He also played a number of non-singing roles, though the basis of his popularity was always his singing. Among his most popular musical films were *Holiday Inn* and *White Christmas*.

Cugat, Xavier (1900–)

Chubby, beaming, Spanish-born bandleader who was identified with the rhumba and became the symbol of Latin American dance music during the 1940s, as far as North American movie audiences were concerned. Among the films he appeared in were *Stage Door Canteen*, *Weekend at the Waldorf* and *Neptune's Daughter*.

Dailey, Dan (1914–1978)

American singer, dancer and actor who had leading roles in many popular musicals during the 1940s and 50s. Some of the films in which he starred were *Mother Wore Tights*, *Give My Regards to Broadway*, *My Blue Heaven*, *Meet Me At The Fair* and *The Girl Next Door*.

Day, Doris (1924–)

Born Doris Mary Anne von Kapelhoff, she started as a band singer and began making movies in the late 1940s. With her short blonde hair, freckles and sunny smile she became a symbol of the 1950s film. Though she was always primarily a singer, she also became known for her non-musical dramatic and comedy roles. Among her most popular musical films were *On Moonlight Bay*, *April in Paris*, *By the Light of the Silvery Moon* and *The Pajama Game*.

Durban, Deanna (1921–)

Canadian-born singer who became an instant success as a teenage star in such films as *Mad About Music*, *First Love*, *Can't Help Singing* and *Up in Central Park*. Her popularity did not survive her youth and she retired in 1948.

Eddy, Nelson (1901–1967)

The most popular hero of the Hollywood operetta during the 1930s. He appeared in eight films with Jeanette MacDonald including *Naughty Marietta*, *Maytime* and *Rose Marie*. His popularity during the 1930s and early 40s was immense, but his reputation as a singer and actor has not survived.

Faye, Alice (1915–)

Born Alice Jeane Leppert, she began as a singer with Rudy Vallee's band and became one of the reigning queens of the Hollywood musical in the late 30s and early 40s, appearing in such lavish productions as *In Old Chicago*, *Alexander's Ragtime Band*, *Rose of Washington Square* and *Hello, Frisco, Hello*.

63

Garland, Judy (1922–1969)

Born Francis Gumm, the child of a vaudeville family, she became a performer at the age of five, and was making movies before she was 14. Whether her well-publicized later emotional problems were due to her treatment as a child star is a matter that has been hotly debated. What is beyond debate is that she was one of the most popular and finest film musical performers ever. Her playing of Dorothy in *The Wizard of Oz* is quite simply one of the best things ever done in a musical. Her musicals with Mickey Rooney were generally lightweight, but in many of her later films such as *The Pirate, Summer Stock, Meet Me in St Louis, The Harvey Girls, In the Good Old Summertime* and *Easter Parade*, she could always be counted on to produce at least one memorable number. She also showed herself to be a more than competent dramatic actress, and as a concert performer she could develop an unsurpassed emotional bond with her audience.

Gaynor, Mitzi (1930–   )

Born Francesca Mitzi de Czanyi von Gerber, she was a leading singer and dancer in musicals during the 1950s. Her biggest success was in *South Pacific*.

Grable, Betty (1916–1973)

She was not only a popular performer during the 1940s, she became practically a symbol of the era, and was the most popular pinup with American servicemen during World War II. She was known as the girl with the million dollar legs, and in fact made a film with that title. Among her many films were *Down Argentine Way, Moon Over Miami, Footlight Serenade, Sweet Rosie O'Grady* and *Mother Wore Tights*.

Grayson, Kathryn (1922–   )

Born Zelma Hendrick. Looked upon as the successor to Jeanette MacDonald, she appeared in such films as *Anchors Aweigh, The Midnight Kiss, Showboat* and *Kiss Me Kate*.

Henie, Sonja (1910–1969)

Norwegian-born Olympic figure skating champion, she appeared in musicals during the 30s and 40s designed to show off her skills on ice. Not surprisingly her films had such titles as *Sun Valley Serenade, Iceland* and *Wintertime*.

Horne, Lena (1917–   )

One of the few black performers to work regularly in Hollywood films during the 1940s and 50s. Even then, aside from specifically black musicals such as *Cabin in the Sky* and *Stormy Weather*, her appearances were limited to specialty numbers, presumably so that they could be easily removed for showing in southern theaters. However, she outlasted those who tried to

64

Judy Garland and Gene Kelly starred in *For Me and My Gal* (1942), a nostalgic romp down the memory lane of pre-World War I vaudeville life.

limit her career, and became a major Broadway star during the 1980s.

Hutton, Betty (1921–   )

Born Elizabeth Thornburg, she became the bouncy leading lady of many Hollywood musicals of the 40s, including *Star Spangled Rhythm* and *And the Angels Sing*. Her best performance was as Annie Oakley in the film version of *Annie Get Your Gun*.

Iturbi, José (1895–1980)

Spanish-born conductor and pianist who appeared in such musicals as *Music for the Millions* and *Anchors Aweigh*. He helped to popularize classical music in films.

Jolson, Al (1886–1950)

Born Asa Yoelson, he had been a celebrated Broadway entertainer when he appeared in the first talking picture *The Jazz Singer*. He became a leading man in musicals from the late 1920s to the mid-40s and then did voiceovers for two film biographies, *The Jolson Story* and *Jolson Sings Again*.

Kaye, Danny (1913–   )

Born David Daniel Kominsky he was an accomplished nightclub performer before he got his first big film break in *Up in Arms*. His enormously popular films of the late 40s and early 50s displayed his comic and musical talents in equal measure.

Keel, Howard (1917–   )

Leading man in many major musicals of the 1950s including *Showboat*, *Kiss Me Kate* and *Seven Brides for Seven Brothers*.

Keeler, Ruby (1909–   )

Petite singer and dancer who appeared in many of the classical musicals of the 1930s, including *42nd Street*, *Gold Diggers of 1933*, *Footlight Parade* and *Go Into Your Dance*. Her most famous partner was Dick Powell, with whom she appeared in seven films.

Kelly, Gene (1912–   )

One of Hollywood's most important musical stars and musical innovators during the 40s and 50s. Though he sang and acted, he was primarily known as a dancer who combined tap, acrobatics and ballet. What audiences were less aware of was that not only did he dance in some of the most innovative musicals ever made in Hollywood, he often choreographed and directed them. Some of the many films in which he did this double duty were *The Pirate*, *Take Me Out to the Ballgame*, *Summer Stock*, *On the Town*, *An American in Paris*, *Singin' in the Rain* and *It's Always Fair Weather*. He appeared with such leading ladies as Judy Garland, Cyd Charisse, Vera-Ellen, Leslie Caron and Debbie Reynolds, but always insisted that his best dancing partner was Fred Astaire. He received a Special Academy Award in 1951.

Lanza, Mario (1921–1959)

Born Alfredo Cocozza, and trained in concert and opera singing before coming to Hollywood. He helped to popularize the operatic style in films, particularly in *The Great Caruso*. His early death was attributed in part to his inability to handle the pressures of movie stardom.

MacDonald, Jeanette (1903–1965)

One-time Broadway leading lady who became the reigning star of the screen operetta during the 1930s. Best known for the films she made with Nelson Eddy.

MacRae, Gordon (1921–   )

Leading man in musicals of the late 1940s and early 50s, including screen adaptations of the Rogers and Hammerstein classics *Oklahoma!* and *Carousel*.

Merman, Ethel (1909–   )

Born Ethel Zimmermann, this brassy and vibrant singer is best known for her Broadway roles, though she did re-create two of them, Reno Sweeny in *Anything Goes* and Sally Adams in *Call Me Madam*, on the screen. She also appeared in a number of other films either as a featured player or in a specialty number.

Miller, Ann (1919–   )

Born Johnnie Collier, she started making low budget musicals in 1937, but by the 1940s she was a leading star of musicals. Known primarily as a tap dancer, she also acted and sang in such films as *On The Town*, *Easter Parade* and *Kiss Me, Kate*. At the age of 60 she once again became a star on Broadway in *Sugar Babies*.

Minnelli, Liza (1946–   )

Daughter of Judy Garland and Vincente Minnelli, she became an authentic star in her own right. Her best-known film is *Cabaret*.

Miranda, Carmen (1909–1955)

Portuguese-born singer and dancer who became known as the 'Brazilian Bombshell' in the films of the 1940s. With her huge fruit-filled hats, six-inch heels and exaggerated accent and movements she was a caricature of the South American 'senhorita'.

O' Brien, Margaret (1937–   )

Child star best remembered for her role in the musical *Meet Me in St Louis*.

Opposite top: Mario Lanza starred in *The Great Caruso* (1950), the movie biography of the great tenor, which had 27 vocal items, including nine opera scenes. The hit popular song was 'The Loveliest Night of the Year.'
Bottom: Left to right: Donald O'Connor, Vera-Ellen, Ethel Merman, George Sanders and Billy De Wolfe in *Call Me Madam* (1953).
Below: Elvis Presley leading a chorus of convicts in a song in *Jailhouse Rock* (1957).

O'Connor, Donald (1925–)

Energetic comedian and song and dance man. He was rarely given a leading role but he made notable appearances in *Singin' in The Rain* and *Call Me Madam* and appeared in dozens of lesser musicals.

Powell, Dick (1904–1963)

Premier juvenile lead of many backstage musicals of the 30s including *42nd Street, Gold Diggers of 1933* and *Footlight Parade*. After his career in musicals ended he successfully turned to playing private-eye roles.

Powell, Jane (1929–)

Born Suzanne Bruce, her small size allowed her to play adolescent parts long after she had ceased to be an adolescent. Her most highly regarded film is *Seven Brides for Seven Brothers*.

Presley, Elvis (1935–1977)

Legendary rock singer who starred in a series of musicals made especially for him. They include *Love Me Tender, Jailhouse Rock, King Creole, GI Blues* and *Paradise Hawaiian Style*.

Reynolds, Debbie (1932–)

One of MGM's adolescent musical stars during the 1950s, she was tapped for the female lead in *Singin' In The Rain*, her memorable musical.

Robeson, Paul (1898–1976)

Black actor and singer best known in musical films for his role in the 1936 version of *Show Boat*.

Robinson, Bill (1878–1949)

Black tap dancer who had attained nearly legendary status and Broadway stardom before he was brought to Hollywood to co-star with Shirley Temple in four movies. He also appeared in a few other movies, including *Stormy Weather* with Lena Horne.

Rogers, Ginger (1911–)

Born Virginia McMath, she appeared on Broadway and in minor musical film roles before teaming up with Fred Astaire in ten films, several of which must be ranked among the all time classics of the musical film. Though best known as a singer and dancer she also appeared successfully in several non-musical films.

Rooney, Mickey (1920–)

Born Joseph Yule Jr, he first appeared on stage in his parents' vaudeville act at the age of two. By the age of six he was appearing in short filmed comedies, and his small size and boyish face allowed him to play juvenile roles for many years. His best known musical films are the series he made with Judy Garland including *Strike up the Band* and *Babes on Broadway*.

Sinatra, Frank (1915–)

Band singer who became a teen-age idol during the 1940s. In films he moved up from brief appearances as a band singer to leading roles in such major musicals as *Anchors Aweigh*, *Take Me Out to the Ball Game*, *On the Town* and *Guys and Dolls*. He won an Oscar for his non-singing role in *From Here to Eternity* in 1953. Since then most of his appearances on the screen have been in nonmusicals.

Streisand, Barbra (1942–)

The major American musical film star of the late 60s, a time when relatively few musical films were being made. Her best known films are adaptations of the Broadway musicals *Funny Girl* and *Hello, Dolly*. She has also appeared in several nonmusical, usually comic, roles.

Temple, Shirley (1928–)

The most popular and successful child star in movie history, she began appearing in films at the age of three. The blonde curly-headed moppet's sentimental films were big box office successes during the depression years. Though most of her films were not straight musicals, she usually was able to sing and dance her way through a few cheery numbers like 'On The Good Ship Lollipop' and 'Animal Crackers in My Soup.' Her film career did not survive her adolescence.

Vallee, Rudy (1901–)

Saxophone-playing band leader and crooner who became a symbol of the 1920s and early 30s. He played the romantic lead in a half dozen or so musicals of that era, but later switched to comic parts and is best remembered for his role in the filmed version of the Broadway hit *How To Succeed in Business Without Really Trying*.

Vera-Ellen (1921–)

Born Vera Ellen Rohe, she started her career as a Broadway dancer and during the late 1940s and 50s she appeared in Hollywood musicals with Gene Kelly, Fred Astaire and Danny Kaye. Her best part was as Ivy Smith in *On The Town*.

Williams, Esther (1921–)

A swimming champion at the age of 15, she was brought to Hollywood as a rival for skating champion Sonja Henie. Though she occasionally emerged from the water to act, she is best known for the splashy aquatic production numbers in films like *On an Island With You*, *Neptune's Daughter*, *Million Dollar Mermaid* and *Jupiter's Darling*.

68

Top : In *High Society* (1956), John Lund is aghast when he discovers that his bride-to-be, Grace Kelly, has gone for a late-night swim with a reporter, Frank Sinatra. The film was a musical version of the play *The Philadelphia Story*, and had such great Cole Porter songs as 'True Love,' 'High Society,' 'Who Wants to Be a Millionaire?' and 'Well, Did Ya Ever?'
Above : Barbra Streisand and Kris Kristofferson starred in a 1976 remake of *A Star Is Born*, the third and worst film version of the story. Updating and transposing the story line from the Hollywood movie world to the 1970s rock music world was a terrible mistake.

Alexander's Ragtime Band
1938 (Fox). D: Henry King. S: Alice Faye, Don Ameche, Ethel Merman, Jack Haley.

All That Jazz
1979 (Fox). D: Bob Fosse. S: Ann Reinking, Ben Vereen.

An American In Paris
1951 (MGM). D: Vincente Minnelli. S: Gene Kelly, Leslie Caron, Oscar Levant.

Anchors Aweigh
1945 (MGM). D: George Sidney. S: Gene Kelly, Frank Sinatra, Kathryn Grayson, José Iturbi.

Annie
1982 (Columbia). D: John Huston. S: Albert Finney, Carol Burnett, Bernadette Peters, Ann Reinking, Aileen Quinn.

Annie Get Your Gun
1950 (MGM). D: George Sidney. S: Betty Hutton, Howard Keel, Keenan Wynn, Benay Venuta.

Applause
1929 (Paramount). D: Rouben Mamoulian. S: Helen Morgan.

Babes In Arms
1939 (MGM). D: Busby Berkeley. S: Mickey Rooney, Judy Garland.

Babes On Broadway
1941 (MGM). D: Busby Berkeley. S: Mickey Rooney, Judy Garland.

Band Wagon, The
1953 (MGM). D: Vincente Minnelli. S: Fred Astaire, Cyd Charisse, Nanette Fabray, Oscar Levant.

Bathing Beauty
1944 (MGM). D: George Sidney. S: Esther Williams, Red Skelton, Basil Rathbone, Harry James and his orchestra.

Bells Are Ringing
1960 (MGM). D: Vincente Minnelli. S: Judy Holliday, Dean Martin, Eddie Foy Jr, Jean Stapleton, Frank Gorshin.

Big Broadcast, The
1932 (Paramount). D: Frank Tuttle. S: Bing Crosby, George Burns, Gracie Allen, Kate Smith.

Billy Rose's Jumbo
1962 (MGM). D: Charles Walters. S: Doris Day, Jimmy Durante, Martha Raye.

Blue Skies
1946 (Paramount). D: Stuart Heisler. S: Bing Crosby, Fred Astaire, Joan Caulfield, Billy De Wolfe.

Brigadoon
1954 (MGM). D: Vincente Minnelli. S: Gene Kelly, Cyd Charisse, Van Johnson.

Filmography

Key: D = director S = stars

Top: All That Jazz (1979) was Bob Fosse's semi-autobiographical musical. Here is a dream sequence during the hero's (Roy Scheider) heart bypass surgery.
Center: Ann Reinking and a group of orphans cheer the strutting of Albert Finney (Daddy Warbucks) and Aileen Quinn in *Annie* (1982).
Above: Bells Are Ringing (1960) told the story of a telephone operator (Judy Holliday) who falls in love with the voice of a client (Dean Martin).

69

Broadway Melody, The
1929 (MGM). D: Harry Beaumont. S: Charles King, Bessie Love.

Broadway Melody of 1940
1940 (MGM). D: Norman Taurog. S: Fred Astaire, Eleanor Powell.

Buddy Holly Story, The
1978 (Columbia). D: Steve Rash. S: Gary Busey.

Bye Bye Birdie
1963 (Columbia). D: George Sidney. S: Dick Van Dyke, Janet Leigh, Ann-Margret, Paul Lynde.

By The Light Of The Silvery Moon
1953 (Warners). D: David Butler. S: Doris Day, Gordon MacRae.

Cabaret
1972 (Allied Artists). D: Bob Fosse. S: Liza Minnelli, Michael York, Joel Grey.

Cabin In The Sky
1943 (MGM). D: Vincente Minnelli. S: Ethel Waters, Eddie Anderson, Lena Horne.

Call Me Madam
1953 (Fox). D: Walter Lang. S: Ethel Merman, George Sanders, Donald O'Connor, Vera-Ellen, Billy De Wolfe, Helmut Dantine, Walter Slezak.

Camelot
1967 (Warners). D: Joshua Logan. S: Richard Harris, Vanessa Redgrave.

Carmen Jones
1954 (Fox). D: Otto Preminger. S: Harry Belafonte, Dorothy Dandridge, Pearl Bailey, Diahann Carroll.

Carousel
1956 (Fox). D: Henry King. S: Gordon MacRae, Shirley Jones, Barbara Ruick.

Coney Island
1943 (Fox). D: Walter Lang. S: Betty Grable, George Montgomery, Cesar Romero, Phil Silvers.

Cover Girl
1944 (Columbia). D: Charles Vidor. S: Rita Hayworth, Gene Kelly, Phil Silvers, Eve Arden.

Daddy Long Legs
1955 (Fox). D: Jean Negulesco. S: Fred Astaire, Leslie Caron, Thelma Ritter.

Dames
1934 (Warners). D: Ray Enright and Busby Berkeley. S: Dick Powell, Ruby Keeler, Joan Blondell, Zasu Pitts, Guy Kibbee.

Damn Yankees
1958 (Warners). D: George Abbott and Stanley Donen. S: Tab Hunter, Gwen Verdon, Jean Stapleton.

Top left and right : Red Skelton dances with Lucille Ball in *Du Barry Was a Lady* (1943).
Opposite center : Some of the Busby Berkeley magic in *Dames* (1934). It was another Powell-Keeler backstage outing. But the plot doesn't matter. The film was an ode to Busby's talents.
Opposite bottom : Nancy Kwan leads a street dance in *Flower Drum Song* (1961), the Rodgers and Hammerstein musical set in the Chinatown of San Francisco.
Above : A scene from *Finian's Rainbow* (1968).

Damsel In Distress, A
1937 (RKO). D: George Stevens. S: Fred Astaire, Joan Fontaine, George Burns, Gracie Allen.

Date With Judy, A
1948 (MGM). D: Richard Thorpe. S: Wallace Beery, Jane Powell, Elizabeth Taylor, Carmen Miranda, Xavier Cugat and his orchestra.

Dolly Sisters, The
1945 (Fox). D: Irving Cummings. S: Betty Grable, John Payne, June Haver, S Z Sakall.

Down Argentine Way
1940 (Fox). D: Irving Cummings. S: Betty Grable, Don Ameche, Carmen Miranda, Charlotte Greenwood, J Carrol Naish.

Du Barry Was A Lady
1943 (MGM). D: Roy Del Ruth. S: Red Skelton, Lucille Ball, Gene Kelly, Virginia O'Brien, Zero Mostel.

Easter Parade
1948 (MGM). D: Charles Walters. S: Fred Astaire, Judy Garland, Peter Lawford, Ann Miller, Keenan Wynn.

Fame
1980 (MGM). D: Alan Parker. S: Irene Cara, Paul McCrane.

Fiddler On The Roof
1971 (United Artists). D: Norman Jewison. S: Topol, Molly Picon.

Finian's Rainbow
1968 (Warners). D: Francis Ford Coppola. S: Fred Astaire, Petula Clark, Tommy Steele, Keenan Wynn.

The Fleet's In
1942 (Paramount). D: Victor Schertzinger. S: Dorothy Lamour, William Holden, Betty Hutton, Eddie Bracken, Cass Daley, Jimmy Dorsey and his band.

Flirtation Walk
1934 (Warners). D: Frank Borzage. S: Dick Powell, Ruby Keeler, Pat O'Brien.

Flower Drum Song
1961 (Universal-International). D: Henry Koster. S: Nancy Kwan, James Shigeta, Juanita Hall, Jack Soo.

Flying Down To Rio
1933 (RKO). D: Thornton Freeland. S: Gene Raymond, Dolores Del Rio, Fred Astaire, Ginger Rogers.

Follow The Fleet
1936 (RKO). D: Mark Sandrich. S: Fred Astaire, Ginger Rogers, Harriet Hilliard, Randolph Scott.

Footlight Parade
1933 (Warners). D: Lloyd Bacon and Busby Berkeley. S: James Cagney, Joan Blondell, Ruby Keeler, Dick Powell.

For Me And My Gal
1942 (MGM). D: Busby Berkeley. S: Judy Garland,
Gene Kelly.

42nd Street
1933 (Warners). D: Lloyd Bacon and Busby Berkeley.
S: Warner Baxter, Dick Powell, Ruby Keeler, Bebe
Daniels, Ginger Rogers, George Brent.

Funny Face
1957 (Paramount). D: Stanley Donen. S: Fred Astaire,
Audrey Hepburn.

Funny Girl
1968 (Columbia). D: William Wyler. S: Barbra
Streisand, Omar Sharif, Ann Francis, Walter Pidgeon.

Gang's All Here, The
1943 (Fox). D: Busby Berkeley. S: Alice Faye, Carmen
Miranda, Charlotte Greenwood, Benny Goodman and
his orchestra.

Gay Desperado, The
1936 (United Artists). D: Rouben Mamoulian. S: Nino
Martini, Ida Lupino, Leo Carrillo, Mischa Auer.

Gay Divorcee, The
1934 (RKO). D: Mark Sandrich. S: Fred Astaire,
Ginger Rogers, Edward Everett Horton, Eric Blore, Erik
Rhodes.

Gentlemen Prefer Blondes
1953 (Fox). D: Howard Hawks. S: Marilyn Monroe,
Jane Russell, Charles Coburn.

George White's Scandals
1934 (Fox). D: George White, Thornton Freeland and
Harry Lachman. S: Rudy Vallee, Jimmy Durante, Alice
Faye, Gregory Ratoff.

George White's 1935 Scandals
1935 (Fox). D: George White. S: Alice Faye, James
Dunn, Eleanor Powell.

Gigi
1958 (MGM). D: Vincente Minnelli. S: Leslie Caron,
Maurice Chevalier, Louis Jourdan, Hermione Gingold.

Girl Crazy
1943 (MGM). D: Norman Taurog and Busby Berkeley.
S: Mickey Rooney, Judy Garland, Nancy Walker, June
Allyson, Tommy Dorsey and his orchestra.

Girl of the Golden West, The
1938 (MGM). D: Robert Z Leonard. S: Jeanette
MacDonald, Nelson Eddy, Walter Pidgeon, Leo
Carrillo, Buddy Ebsen.

Glenn Miller Story, The
1954 (Universal). D: Anthony Mann. S: James Stewart,
June Allyson, Henry Morgan, Phil Harris.

Go Into Your Dance
1935 (Warners). D: Archie Mayo. S: Al Jolson, Ruby
Keeler, Glenda Farrell, Helen Morgan, Patsy Kelly.

Opposite top : Warner Baxter gives Ruby Keeler a hard time at a rehearsal in *Forty-Second Street* (1933). To the left of Keeler is Una Merkel; to the right of Baxter is Ginger Rogers.
Opposite center : John Travolta in *Grease* (1978).
Bottom : Nino Martini (center) in a Western musical—*The Gay Desperado* (1936).
Below : Hair (1979) was a musical adaptation of the long-running Broadway show about the flower children of the 1960s. It had some fine songs, such as 'The Age of Aquarius.'

Gold Diggers Of Broadway, The
1929 (Warners). D: Roy Del Ruth. S: Nancy Welford, Conway Tearle.

Gold Diggers Of 1933
1933 (Warners). D: Mervyn LeRoy and Busby Berkeley. S: Dick Powell, Joan Blondell, Ruby Keeler, Guy Kibbee, Ginger Rogers.

Gold Diggers Of 1937
1936 (Warners). D: Lloyd Bacon. S: Dick Powell, Joan Blondell, Victor Moore, Glenda Farrell.

Good News
1948 (MGM). D: Charles Walters. S: June Allyson, Peter Lawford, Mel Torme.

Grease
1978 (Paramount). D: Randal Kleiser. S: John Travolta, Olivia Newton-John, Stockard Channing, Eve Arden, Frankie Avalon, Joan Blondell, Sid Caesar, Alice Ghostley.

Great Caruso, The
1951 (MGM). D: Richard Thorpe. S: Mario Lanza, Ann Blyth, Dorothy Kirsten.

Great Ziegfeld, The
1936 (MGM). D: Robert Z Leonard. S: William Powell, Myrna Loy, Luise Rainer, Frank Morgan, Ray Bolger.

Guys And Dolls
1955 (Samuel Goldwyn Production, MGM). D: Joseph L Mankiewicz. S: Marlon Brando, Frank Sinatra, Jean Simmons, Vivian Blaine, Stubby Kaye.

Gypsy
1962 (Warners). D: Mervyn LeRoy. S: Rosalind Russell, Natalie Wood, Karl Malden.

Hair
1979 (United Artists). D: Milos Forman. S: John Savage, Treat Williams, Charlotte Rae.

Happy Days
1930 (Fox). D: Benjamin Stoloff. S: Janet Gaynor, Will Rogers, Charles Farrell, Victor McLaglen, Dixie Lee.

Harvey Girls, The
1946 (MGM). D: George Sidney. S: Judy Garland, John Hodiak, Angela Lansbury, Marjorie Main, Virginia O'Brien, Cyd Charisse, Ray Bolger, Kenny Baker.

Hello, Dolly!
1969 (Fox). D: Gene Kelly. S: Barbra Streisand, Walter Matthau, Tommy Tune, Louis Armstrong.

Hello, Frisco, Hello
1943 (Fox). D: Bruce Humberstone. S: Alice Faye, John Payne, Jack Oakie, Lynn Bari, June Havoc, Ward Bond.

High Society
1956 (MGM). D: Charles Walters. S: Bing Crosby,

Grace Kelly, Frank Sinatra, Celeste Holm, Louis Armstrong.

High, Wide And Handsome
1937 (Paramount). D: Rouben Mamoulian. S: Irene Dunne, Randolph Scott, Dorothy Lamour, Akim Tamiroff.

Holiday Inn
1942 (Paramount). D: Mark Sandrich. S: Bing Crosby, Fred Astaire, Marjorie Reynolds.

Hollywood Revue Of 1929, The
1929 (MGM). D: Charles F Riesner. S: Jack Benny, Conrad Nagel, Joan Crawford, Marion Davies, Laurel and Hardy, Marie Dressler, Buster Keaton, Norma Shearer, John Gilbert.

Honey
1930 (Paramount). D: Wesley Ruggles. S: Nancy Carroll, Lillian Roth, Skeets Gallagher, ZaSu Pitts.

Honeymoon Hotel
1937 (Warners). D: Busby Berkeley. S: Dick Powell, Rosemary Lane, Glenda Farrell, Frances Langford, Benny Goodman and his orchestra.

How To Succeed In Business Without Really Trying
1967 (United Artists). D: David Swift. S: Robert Morse, Rudy Vallee, Michele Lee.

I Married An Angel
1942 (MGM). D: W S Van Dyke II. S: Jeanette MacDonald, Nelson Eddy.

In The Good Old Summertime
1949 (MGM). D: Robert Z Leonard. S: Judy Garland, Van Johnson, Spring Byington.

Jailhouse Rock
1957 (MGM). D: Richard Thorpe. S: Elvis Presley.

Jazz Singer, The
1927 (Warners). D: Alan Crosland. S: Al Jolson, Eugenie Besserer, Warner Oland.

Jazz Singer, The
1980 (Associated Film Distribution). D: Richard Fleischer. S: Neil Diamond, Laurence Olivier, Lucie Arnaz.

Jesus Christ, Superstar
1973 (Universal). D: Norman Jewison. S: Ted Neeley, Yvonne Elliman, Joshua Mostel.

Jolson Story, The
1946 (Columbia). D: Alfred E Green. S: Larry Parks, Evelyn Keyes.

Kid From Brooklyn, The
1946 (RKO Radio). D: Norman Z McLeod. S: Danny Kaye, Virginia Mayo, Vera-Ellen, Walter Abel.

King And I, The
1956 (Fox). D: Walter Lang. S: Deborah Kerr, Yul Brynner, Rita Moreno.

Opposite top : A scene from the pitiful remake of *The Jazz Singer* (1980) with Lucie Arnaz and Neil Diamond.
Opposite center : The circus scene from *Lady in the Dark* (1944), starring Ginger Rogers.
Bottom : MacDonald and Eddy singing in *Maytime* (1937), a schmaltzy film that was the biggest moneymaker that year—worldwide. The story was about the romance between an opera prima donna and a baritone.
Below : A Scene from *Jesus Christ, Superstar* (1973).

Kiss Me, Kate
1953 (MGM). D: George Sidney. S: Kathryn Grayson, Howard Keel, Ann Miller, Bob Fosse, James Whitmore, Keenan Wynn.

Lady In The Dark
1944 (Paramount). D: Mitchell Leisen. S: Ginger Rogers, Ray Milland, Warner Baxter, Mischa Auer, Barry Sullivan.

Lili
1953 (MGM). D: Charles Walters. S: Leslie Caron, Mel Ferrer, Jean Pierre Aumont, Zsa Zsa Gabor, Kurt Kaznar, Amanda Blake.

Lillian Russell
1940 (Fox). D: Irving Cummings. S: Alice Faye, Don Ameche, Henry Fonda, Edward Arnold, Nigel Bruce.

Love Parade, The
1929 (Paramount). D: Ernst Lubitsch. S: Maurice Chevalier, Jeanette MacDonald, Lupino Lane, Lillian Roth.

Lullaby Of Broadway
1951 (Warners). D: David Butler. S: Doris Day, Gene Nelson, S Z Sakall, Billy De Wolfe.

Mame
1974 (Warners). D: Gene Saks. S: Lucille Ball, Bea Arthur, Robert Preston.

Mary Poppins
1964 (A Walt Disney Production released by Buena Vista). D: Robert Stevenson. S: Julie Andrews, Dick Van Dyke, David Tomlinson, Glynis Johns, Ed Wynn, Arthur Treacher, Karen Dotrice.

Maytime
1937 (MGM). D: Robert Z Leonard. S: Jeanette MacDonald, Nelson Eddy, John Barrymore.

Meet Me In St Louis
1944 (MGM). D: Vincente Minnelli. S: Judy Garland, Margaret O'Brien, Mary Astor, Marjorie Main.

Merry Widow, The
1934 (MGM). D: Ernst Lubitsch. S: Maurice Chevalier, Jeanette MacDonald, Edward Everett Horton.

Merry Widow, The
1952 (MGM). D: Curtis Bernhardt. S: Lana Turner, Fernando Lamas, Una Merkel.

Moon Over Miami
1941 (Fox). D: Walter Lang. S: Betty Grable, Don Ameche, Robert Cummings, Charlotte Greenwood, Carole Landis, Jack Haley.

Mother Wore Tights
1947 (Fox). D: Walter Lang. S: Betty Grable, Dan Dailey, Mona Freeman.

Music For Millions
1944 (MGM). D: Henry Koster. S: June Allyson, Margaret O'Brien, José Iturbi, Jimmy Durante, Marie Wilson.

Music Man, The
1962 (Warners). D: Morton Da Costa. S: Robert Preston, Shirley Jones, Buddy Hackett, Hermione Gingold.

My Fair Lady
1964 (Warners). D: George Cukor. S: Rex Harrison, Audrey Hepburn, Stanley Holloway, Gladys Cooper.

My Sister Eileen
1955 (Columbia). D: Richard Quine. S: Betty Garrett, Janet Leigh, Jack Lemon, Bob Fosse, Kurt Kaznar.

Naughty Marietta
1935 (MGM). D: W S Van Dyke II. S: Nelson Eddy, Jeanette MacDonald, Frank Morgan, Elsa Lanchester.

Neptune's Daughter
1949 (MGM). D: Edward Buzzell. S: Esther Williams, Red Skelton, Ricardo Montalban, Betty Garrett, Keenan Wynn, Xavier Cugat and his orchestra.

New Moon
1940 (MGM). D: Robert Z Leonard. S: Jeanette MacDonald, Nelson Eddy.

Night And Day
1946 (Warners). D: Michael Curtiz. S: Cary Grant, Alexis Smith, Monty Woolley, Ginny Simms, Jane Wyman, Eve Arden, Mary Martin.

Oklahoma!
1955 (An Arthur N Hornblow Production, released by Magna Theater Corporation). D: Fred Zinnemann. S: Gordon MacRae, Shirley Jones.

Oliver!
1968 (Columbia). D: Carol Reed. S: Ron Moody, Oliver Reed, Hugh Griffith.

On A Clear Day You Can See Forever
1970 (Paramount). D: Vincente Minnelli. S: Barbra Streisand, Yves Montand, Bob Newhart, Jack Nicholson.

On An Island With You
1948 (MGM). D: Richard Thorpe. S: Esther Williams, Peter Lawford, Ricardo Montalban, Jimmy Durante, Cyd Charisse, Xavier Cugat and his orchestra.

One Hour With You
1932 (Paramount). D: Ernst Lubitsch. S: Maurice Chevalier, Jeanette MacDonald, Charles Ruggles, Roland Young.

One In A Million
1936 (Fox). D: Sidney Lanfield. S: Sonja Henie, Adolphe Menjou, Don Ameche, Jean Hersholt, the Ritz Brothers, Dixie Dunbar, Borrah Minnevitch.

One Night Of Love
1934 (Columbia). D: Victor Schertzinger. S: Grace Moore, Tullio Carminati, Lyle Talbot.

On The Town
1949 (MGM). D: Stanley Donen and Gene Kelly. S: Gene Kelly, Frank Sinatra, Jules Munshin, Vera-Ellen, Betty Garrett, Ann Miller.

Pajama Game, The
1957 (Warners). D: George Abbott and Stanley Donen. S: Doris Day, John Raitt, Carol Haney, Eddie Foy Jr.

Pal Joey
1957 (Columbia). D: George Sidney. S: Frank Sinatra, Rita Hayworth, Kim Novak.

Panama Hattie
1942 (MGM). D: Norman Z McLeod. S: Ann Sothern, Dan Dailey, Red Skelton, Virginia O'Brien, Rags Ragland.

Pennies From Heaven
1936 (Columbia). D: Norman Z McLeod. S: Bing Crosby, Madge Evans, Louis Armstrong and his orchestra.

Pennies From Heaven
1981 (MGM). D: Herb Ross. S: Steve Martin, Bernadette Peters.

Pin Up Girl
1944 (Fox). D: Bruce Humberstone. S: Betty Grable, Martha Raye, Joe E Brown.

Pirate, The
1948 (MGM). D: Vincente Minnelli. S: Judy Garland, Gene Kelly, Walter Slezak, Gladys Cooper.

Poor Little Rich Girl
1936 (Fox). D: Irving Cummings. S: Shirley Temple.

Porgy And Bess
1959 (A Samuel Goldwyn Production, released by Columbia). D: Otto Preminger. S: Sidney Poitier, Dorothy Dandridge, Sammy Davis Jr, Pearl Bailey. Brock Peters, Diahann Carroll.

Rhapsody In Blue
1945 (Warners). D: Irving Rapper. S: Robert Alda, Joan Leslie, Alexis Smith, Charles Coburn, Oscar Levant, Rosemary DeCamp, Morris Carnovsky.

Rhythm On The Range
1936 (Paramount). D: Norman Taurog. S: Bing Crosby, Frances Farmer, Martha Raye.

Roberta
1935 (RKO). D: William A Seiter. S: Fred Astaire, Ginger Rogers, Irene Dunne, Randolph Scott.

Rose, The
1979 (Fox). D: Mark Rydell. S: Bette Midler, Alan Bates.

Top : A romantic moment for Barbra Streisand in *On a Clear Day You Can See Forever* (1970).

Center : Bette Midler in *The Rose* (1979), in which she played a hard-rock superstar.

Above : John Kerr, Mitzie Gaynor and Rossano Brazzi in a tense moment from *South Pacific* (1958).

Rose Marie
1936 (MGM). D: W S Van Dyke II. S: Jeanette MacDonald, Nelson Eddy, James Stewart, Allan Jones.

Royal Wedding
1951 (MGM). D: Stanley Donen. S: Fred Astaire, Jane Powell, Peter Lawford, Sarah Churchill, Keenan Wynn.

Sally
1929 (Warners). D: John Francis Dillon. S: Marilyn Miller, Joe E Brown.

Seven Brides For Seven Brothers
1954 (MGM). D: Stanley Donen. S: Jane Powell, Howard Keel, Julie Newmar, Russ Tamblyn.

Shall We Dance?
1937 (RKO). D: Mark Sandrich. S: Fred Astaire, Ginger Rogers, Edward Everett Horton, Eric Blore.

Show Boat
1951 (MGM). D: George Sidney. S: Kathryn Grayson, Howard Keel, Marge and Gower Champion, Ava Gardner, Joe E Brown, Agnes Moorehead, William Warfield.

Silk Stockings
1957 (MGM). D: Rouben Mamoulian. S: Fred Astaire, Cyd Charisse, Janis Paige, Peter Lorre, Jules Munshin.

Singing Fool, The
1928 (Warners). D: Lloyd Bacon. S: Al Jolson, Betty Bronson.

Singin' In The Rain
1952 (MGM). D: Stanley Donen and Gene Kelly. S: Gene Kelly, Debbie Reynolds, Donald O'Connor, Jean Hagen, Millard Mitchell, Cyd Charisse.

Small Town Girl
1953 (MGM). D: Leslie Kardos. S: Jane Powell, Farley Granger, Ann Miller, Chill Wills, S Z Sakall, Fay Wray.

Song Of The South
1946 (A Walt Disney Production, released by RKO). D: Wilfred Jackson and Harve Foster. S: Ruth Warrick, James Baskett, Bobby Driscoll, Luana Patten.

Sound Of Music, The
1965 (Fox). D: Robert Wise. S: Julie Andrews, Christopher Plummer, Eleanor Parker, Peggy Wood.

South Pacific
1958 (Fox). D: Joshua Logan. S: Mitzi Gaynor, Rossano Brazzi, France Nuyen, Juanita Hall.

Stand Up And Cheer
1934 (Fox). D: Hamilton MacFadden. S: Warner Baxter, Shirley Temple, Aunt Jemima.

Star Is Born, A
1954 (Warners). D: George Cukor. S: Judy Garland, James Mason, Jack Carson, Charles Bickford, Tommy Noonan.

Star Is Born, A
1976 (Warners). D: Frank Pierson. S: Barbra Streisand, Kris Kristofferson, Gary Busey.

State Fair
1945 (Fox). D: Walter Lang. S: Jeanne Crain, Dana Andrews, Dick Haymes, Vivian Blaine, Fay Bainter.

Stormy Weather
1943 (Fox). D: Andrew Stone. S: Bill Robinson, Lena Horne, Cab Calloway and his band, Fats Waller.

Strike Up The Band
1940 (MGM). D: Busby Berkeley. S: Mickey Rooney, Judy Garland, Paul Whiteman.

Sunny Side Up
1929 (Fox). D: David Butler. S: Janet Gaynor, Charles Farrell.

Sweet Charity
1969 (Universal). D: Bob Fosse. S: Shirley MacLaine, Ricardo Montalban, Sammy Davis Jr, Chita Rivera, Stubby Kaye.

Sweethearts
1938 (MGM). D: W S Van Dyke II. S: Jeanette MacDonald, Nelson Eddy, Frank Morgan, Ray Bolger, Mischa Auer.

Sweet Rosy O'Grady
1943 (Fox). D: Irving Cummings. S: Betty Grable, Robert Young, Adolphe Menjou.

Swing Time
1936 (RKO). D: George Stevens. S: Fred Astaire, Ginger Rogers, Victor Moore, Eric Blore, Betty Furness.

Take Me Out To The Ball Game
1949 (MGM). D: Busby Berkeley. S: Gene Kelly, Esther Williams, Frank Sinatra, Betty Garrett, Jules Munshin, Edward Arnold.

That Night In Rio
1941 (Fox). D: Irving Cummings. S: Alice Faye, Don Ameche, Carmen Miranda, S Z Sakall, J Carrol Naish.

There's No Business Like Show Business
1954 (Fox). D: Walter Lang. S: Ethel Merman, Dan Dailey, Mitzi Gaynor, Marilyn Monroe, Donald O'Connor, Johnnie Ray.

This Is The Army
1943 (Warners). D: Michael Curtiz. S: George Murphy, Ronald Reagan, Joan Leslie, Kate Smith, Frances Langford, Joe Louis, Irving Berlin.

Thousands Cheer
1943 (MGM). D: George Sidney. S: Kathryn Grayson, Gene Kelly, Mary Astor.

Three Caballeros, The
1945 (A Walt Disney Production, released by RKO Radio). D: Norman Ferguson. S: Aurora Miranda,

Opposite top: One of Judy Garland's great roles—as Vicki Lester in *A Star Is Born* (1954), the remake of the nonmusical of 1937. Judy was at her pinnacle singing 'Born in a Trunk' and 'The Man That Got Away.'
Below: The Wiz (1978) was a fanciful remake of *The Wizard of Oz* and starred Diana Ross.
Bottom: The 'Hey, Big Spender' routine from *Sweet Charity* (1969), an adaptation of Fellini's film *Nights of Cabiria* (1957). It is the story of a dance hall hostess (Shirley MacLaine, center, rear) with the proverbial heart of gold. Among the Cy Coleman-Dorothy Fields songs were 'If They Could See Me Now' and 'Rhythm of Life.'

Carmen Molina, Trio Calaveras, voices of Sterling Holloway, Clarence Nash, José Oliveira.

Three Little Words
1950 (MGM). D: Richard Thorpe. S: Fred Astaire, Vera-Ellen, Red Skelton, Arlene Dahl, Debbie Reynolds, Gloria De Haven.

Toast Of New Orleans, The
1950 (MGM). D: Norman Taurog. S: Mario Lanza, Kathryn Grayson, David Niven, J Carrol Naish.

Top Hat
1935 (RKO). D: Mark Sandrich. S: Fred Astaire, Ginger Rogers, Edward Everett Horton, Helen Broderick, Eric Blore, Erik Rhodes.

Up In Arms
1944 (A Samuel Goldwyn Production, released by RKO Radio). D: Elliot Nugent. S: Danny Kaye, Dinah Shore, Dana Andrews.

We're Not Dressing
1934 (Paramount). D: Norman Taurog. S: Bing Crosby, Carole Lombard, George Burns, Gracie Allen, Ethel Merman, Ray Milland.

West Side Story
1961 (United Artists). D: Robert Wise and Jerome Robbins. S: Natalie Wood, Rita Moreno, Russ Tamblyn.

Where's Charley?
1952 (Warners). D: David Butler. S: Ray Bolger, Allyn McLerie.

White Christmas
1954 (Paramount). D: Michael Curtiz. S: Bing Crosby, Danny Kaye, Rosemary Clooney, Vera-Ellen.

Whoopee
1930 (A Samuel Goldwyn Production, released by United Artists). D: Thornton Freeland. S: Eddie Cantor, Eleanor Hunt, Betty Grable.

Wiz, The
1978 (Universal). D: Sidney Lumet. S: Diana Ross, Michael Jackson, Nipsey Russell, Mabel King, Richard Pryor, Lena Horne.

Wizard Of Oz, The
1939 (MGM). D: Victor Fleming. S: Judy Garland, Bert Lahr, Ray Bolger, Jack Haley, Frank Morgan, Margaret Hamilton, Billie Burke.

Yankee Doodle Dandy
1942 (Warners). D: Michael Curtiz. S: James Cagney, Walter Huston, Joan Leslie, Rosemary DeCamp.

Ziegfeld Girl
1941 (MGM). D: Robert Z Leonard. S: Lana Turner, James Stewart, Hedy Lamarr, Judy Garland, Tony Martin, Jackie Cooper, Eve Arden, Dan Dailey.

INDEX

ACKNOWLEDGMENTS

The author and publisher would like to thank the following people who have helped in the preparation of this book: Abigail Sturgis, who designed it; Thomas G Aylesworth, who edited it; John K Crowley, who did the photo research; Cynthia Klein, who prepared the index.

PICTURE CREDITS

Museum of Modern Art: 4–5, 8 (bottom), 9 (top right), 10–11, 12 (bottom), 14–15, 16–17, 18, 19 (top), 20, 21, 22–23, 26, 27, 28–29, 29, 32, 33 (top), 34 (bottom), 35, 37, 38, 39, 40 (top), 41 (bottom), 44 (top), 45 (bottom), 46 (top left), 47, 48, 49 (top), 52 (top), 53, 56, 57 (top right and left), 59 (bottom), 60, 61, 62, 63 (top), 66, 67, 68 (top), 70 (top), 71 (top), 72 (top), 74, 75.
Jerry Ohlinger's Movie Material Store: 1, 6 (inset), 8 (top left), 17 (inset), 24, 32–33, 33, 34 (top), 36–37 (top), 40 (bottom), 41 (top), 42–43, 45 (top), 46 (top right), 49 (bottom left and right), 50, 57 (bottom right), 64–65, 66–67, 69 (center and bottom), 70 (bottom), 72 (center), 73 (top), 77 (center), 78 (top), 79 (top).
National Film Archive: 2, 8–9, 12 (top), 13, 19 (bottom), 25, 33 (bottom), 36–37 (bottom), 44 (bottom), 46 (bottom), 49, 52 (bottom), 54–55, 59 (top), 63 (center and bottom), 68 (bottom), 69 (top), 70 (center), 71 (bottom), 72–73, 77 (top and bottom), 78–79.
Bill Yenne: 6–7, 51.